Praise for *Discovering*

Chris Scott is skilled and anointed to help you discover and develop your spiritual gifts. God has given her wisdom and insight in this particular area so that every believer discovers their potential in Christ. This book will help you discover your purpose in God as you discover the spiritual gifts on the inside of you.

Pastor T.J. McBride, Senior Pastor
Tabernacle of Praise Church International

Master Coach, Chris Scott has used her God given interpretation to give clarity and understanding to Discovering Your Spiritual Gifts. She has placed great emphasis on the process in which God takes us all through to perfect and purify those things that allow for the "Gifts" to flow. There has been placed great value not so much on the "Gift" although it is important for the Body of Christ to as she has so clearly stated that "Discovering your Spiritual Gifts is a Process". What has been placed into context is, "the process." In a most dynamic way this instructional book has been laid out in sections, paragraphs and chapters and will not only give light to what God has originally intended for us as it relates to discovering, understanding imparting, and illustrating the spiritual gifts but this book is also a roadmap for generations

to follow. It can be used in Ministry School, Sunday School, Eldership classes and New Member classes. This tool can also be easily used as a Workbook to further explain to the Body of Christ how important it is to stay the course in the process and the journey that one must take in order to fully be operational and effective in our spiritual gifts to glorify God in every good work. Hebrews 13:21 Jubilee Bible 2000 states "make you perfect in every good work to do his will, working in you that which is well pleasing in his sight, through Jesus Christ, to whom be glory for the ages of the ages."

Amen.

Janice L. Parks,

Empowerment Speaker, Author and Certified Holistic Life Coach

DISCOVERING YOUR

Spiritual Gifts

CONNECTING THE DOTS TO YOUR PURPOSE

BY CHRIS SCOTT

Scott, Chris

www.chrisscott.net

ISBN: 978-0692124192 (paperback)

ASIN: B07K6WC852 (eBook)

Book Production and Editing by Publish and Promote

Design and layout by Publish and Promote

Cover design by Trevor Bailey

DEDICATION

This book is dedicated to loving memory of
Russell P. Williamson, my father
and
Joycelyn P. Gilbert-Williamson-Parillon, my mother
The best parents I could ever ask for.
Thank you for leaving a Legacy that I will forever cherish
Missing and loving you always!

TABLE OF CONTENTS

FOREWORD
By Dr. Patricia Bailey

Making your callings and elections sure is the pivot axle that your hidden potential rest upon. Many people go throughout their entire life never discovering their predestined abilities. Unfortunately, many are sitting in church every Sunday morning. The author has done a superb job of helping you to navigate your path of discovering and developing the best asset known to a believer, and this is your gifting. This book goes far beyond literary accuracy and instruction. The book is instructional yet inspirational. It's spiritual yet practical. It's applicable yet leaves you with the challenge of believing that what was given to me is beyond me. Chris has skillfully provided for you a road map to your destiny. She's given you the tools and coupled that with a baited expectation to believe in your gift. After reading the book you leave with the audacity of hope that she awakened in you through this book. There is no doubt that the Spirit of God brooded over her as she penned the eternal thoughts of God towards you as the Father has dealt to every man the gift according to the Fathers design for each significant person. You can't afford to waste another moment of your valued life without knowing and confirming your gift and then moving forward to develop and maximize your gift. What a shame and reproach to God to be given such a treasure wrapped and packaged in your gift and then never unveil the gift. The one who is the express glory of God has given himself as a ransom so that you could house the very gifts given and distributed by the Almighty.

This book will give you a new perspective of your life's new horizon. The rebirth of your optimum life is within the pages of this book. Chris has done an incredible job of painting a tapestry of expectation that is released and manifested through operating within your gifting. Your gift was given to maximize your life. Your gift was given to take the struggle out of your life. This book is a must-read; that is if you are ready to take on the challenge of living a greater life that's trapped in the substratum of YOUR GIFT.

ACKNOWLEDGEMENT

My praise to God for imparting wisdom, knowledge and understanding in me and giving me the courage to become bold in my spiritual journey. I thank my amazing husband A.C. for being a loving, caring provider to our children for more than three decades. You have blessed my life in ways that I may not have yet shared. Even as I write these words, I am watching you sleep and be patient with me through the noise of the clicking computer keys. Thank you for believing in me and encouraging me to write this book. You are truly a wonderful man of the most High God. Your early morning prayers, way before the break of dawn, helped carry me through many days.

Thank you to my firstborn child ChelleyAnn, who bared the newness of parenthood, before your dad and I knew how to be parents. You continue to make me proud.

Thank you to my loving daughter Samantha for always being kind and loving to me. You are an amazing mother and wife. You make me proud each day.

To my only son Andrew, you are caring, kind-hearted and a strong man like your father and I am proud of your accomplishments. You may have never heard of my experience noted in this book but thank you for allowing me to share. Loving you always.

Thank you to my Pastor T.J. McBride for pushing and stretching me to do what God has called me to do. Your empowering words have never fallen on deaf ears. Thank you to my amazing missions mentor Dr. Patricia Bailey for always pouring into me and giving me insight and wisdom.

INTRODUCTION

For we are labourers together with God: ye are God's husbandry, ye are God's building. 1 Corinthians 3:9

I t's been a passion of mine for as long as I can remember to help people answer the question "what on earth am I here for". It is a frustrating place to be, not knowing who you are and what your purpose is while here on this earth. The desire to help others connect the dots has lead me to write this book. When you know what your gifts are, several things begin to happen. Knowing your spiritual gifts will allow you to clearly understand what God wants for your life. It is imperative to know that He has entrusted us with these gifts, therefore there has to be a reason, right? Why would God even bother with giving us these gifts?

> *"You are the salt of the earth. But if the salt loses its saltiness, how can it be made salty again? It is no longer good for anything, except to be thrown out and trampled underfoot. Matthew 5:13*

Knowing our gifts help us to be the salt and light of the earth. Utilizing our gifts is us being the salt and light to others.

When we are not operating effectively in our spiritual gifts then we are like the later part of this scripture and not living with real purpose. When we operate in the gift that God has given to us freely, then we will be able to know how the Holy Spirit is operating in us.

This book will help you to know how to "stay in your lane". When you know your gifts, you will be the best you can be. You won't try to be like everyone else and your level of success will be heightened and inevitable. You will be able to walk in boldness and clarity through this journey called life. As you read these chapters, a light bulb will go off when you recognize yourself in your gifts. Knowing your spiritual gifts will also help you in the secular world. You will find that you are more effective in your day to day professional life. You will no longer find yourself serving in areas that don't match your gifts.

Knowing your spiritual gifts will help fill and empty void and help fill the desire that God has placed in you. This fulfillment will help you unify with other Christians because spiritual gifts complement each other. You have a place in ministry and life period! Once you are operating in your spiritual gifts, you will begin to live on purpose and be better equipped to fill the calling on your life.

When you know your gifts and are walking in your area of calling, your level of confidence, self-esteem and self-acceptance will be mastered! Enjoy!

CHAPTER 1

DISCOVERING YOUR SPIRITUAL GIFTS IS A PROCESS

"There are some things so dear, some things so precious, some things so eternally true, that they are worth dying for. And I submit to you that if a man has not discovered something that he will die for, he isn't fit to live."
Dr. Martin Luther King Jr.

I am glad that you have decided to take this step to discovering or confirming your spiritual gifts. To truly live out the purpose God has placed us on earth for, we must know what they are. In addition to knowing what they are, we must also use these gifts to help others. God did not entrust us with these important gifts to help ourselves, but rather help others. Paul speaks of spiritual gifts in Romans 1:11-12 where he states, *"I long to see you so that I may impart to you some spiritual gift to make you strong— that is, that you and I may be mutually encouraged by each other's faith."* Paul spoke of his gift and wanting to impart to the people to make them more powerful. I believe that Paul wanted to impart his gifts of wisdom, knowledge, teaching and much more. Some could misinterpret these gifts as physical items, but they were spiritual. Spiritual gifts outweigh physical gifts by far.

Throughout this book, I will share stories of how God stirs up our gifts and takes us through the process of spiritual transformation as we grow in Christ.

By the end of this book, I believe the Holy Spirit would have moved in you to help you not just discover or confirm your spiritual gifts, but you will begin to operate in them and your gifts operate in you. Trust me. Do not stress anymore about finding your purpose in life. God has answered your prayer by leading you to read this book. The dots will begin to connect for you and you will no longer have to ask the question "What on earth am I here for?"

Your life with God should be one of joy and peace in Him. I can't imagine what I did without truly knowing Him. "I was once lost, but now I am found" as the songwriter says. The Christian growth is continuous and must be consistent and thereby a journey to discovering our spiritual gifts. Each day our relationship with Christ should grow. We must continue to tell and show God how much we love Him. In return, He will talk to us through the Holy Spirit. Knowing your spiritual gifts will allow you to continue to walk in love with your fellowman, Christians and non-Christians alike.

We are to love everyone with the love of God and use those gifts to show that love.

If you don't know Christ and you want a relationship with Him for yourself, stop and say this prayer below. You will notice that the prayer is mentioned again in the book, as you may not be ready to accept Christ now. However, I admonish you to surrender to His purpose in your life. You are valuable to God and He loves you so much that He guided me to write this book with you in mind.

Prayer of Salvation

"Father, in Jesus' Name, I thank you now for another opportunity that you have allowed me to come before your presence. I ask you now to forgive me of all my sins. Forgive me for anything I've done or anything I have said that has brought shame to your Holy Name. I confess with my mouth and I believe in my heart that God has raised Jesus from the dead and He now lives in me. Thank You Lord that I am saved, and I will serve you for the rest of my life." In Jesus' Name. Amen.

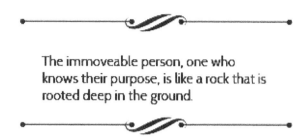

The immoveable person, one who
knows their purpose, is like a rock that is
rooted deep in the ground.

Spiritual Growth

Spiritual formation takes place as we use our spiritual gifts
to glorify God. Spiritual formation is our growth in Christ.
This does not take place overnight but over some time and
continuously. You are also not always going to see growth
immediately. But one day as you look back over your life you
will see the changes. You see, the opportunity for spiritual
growth as we use our gifts began when God allowed Jesus to
take our place and grant us the chance for eternal life. The
spiritual process continues as we use our gifts and speaks of
admonition and the announcement that God is living in us
each day. Paul tells the Corinthians to remain in faith and
hope, no matter what things may look like. This is the only
way that spiritual growth can exist. We must stay in Christ
and Christ in us to continue to grow each day.

1 Corinthians 15:58 says *"Therefore, my beloved brethren,
be ye steadfast, unmovable, always abounding in the work of*

the Lord, forasmuch as ye know that your labour is not in vain in the Lord." This means that we must remain spiritually grounded in Christ. In researching the word steadfast I gained a better understanding of spiritual growth. You see, someone that is steadfast requires action. Someone that is steadfast is convinced that whatever they are doing is the right way to do it and they refuse to give up or change. That sounds like a committed person. The word immoveable is also important because it means an attitude that cannot be easily changed. These two words come about when you have gained true confidence in who you are and confidence in the gifts that God has placed inside of you.

The immoveable person, one who knows their purpose, is like a rock that is rooted deep in the ground. Similar to us being able to see the top portion of a glacier, but can't see that the surface underneath expands far and wide. That glacier is immoveable, just like when we are rooted and grounded in God and operating in our gifts.

Paul mentions to the people of Corinth the need to remain steadfast and immovable because they had to be aware of false doctrine and false teaching. When someone believes what they believe and stand firm on it, they cannot be easily swayed by others. It is imperative that gifts are not misused to manipulate others. When we discover and start to operate in our spiritual gifts, we must die to the flesh and come alive again to the Spirit. This is all part of spiritual growth in Christ. We as Christians must have a will to want a relationship with Christ and thereby grow in our walk by making a difference in the lives of others.

The word transformation is considered a radical action of God in us. God transforms us and makes us new again in Him. The old things are passed away and things are new. We must however maintain and sustain the things of God as we walk the journey of spiritual growth. This change does not come overnight, but it does happen. The change is sometimes noticeable and at other times not seen until much later on in our walk as the use of our gifts becomes more evident. Let's start connecting the dots by looking at my journey.

The Journey

> *"Many are the plans in a person's heart, but it is the Lord's purpose that prevails" (Proverbs 19:21).*

Again, it is important to understand that discovering your gifts, passion and purpose does not come overnight. There are times that we operate in our gifts and don't even realize that we are doing just that. When I was younger, we lived in Queens, New York, in a three-story home on the second floor. We had tenants on the third floor where my parents rented out rooms from time to time. My siblings and I saw many tenants move in and out during the time we lived there. I was always glad whenever a family with children moved in. Since my parents were super strict and did not allow us to go anywhere or have friends, the tenants were a way of me having playmates. They were who I needed to be able to operate in my gifts. I could remember having the children of the tenants meet me in the basement for class. At 10 years old, I started teaching/pretending to be a teacher and taught my first class. I would line up chairs and create a desk area for myself and teach on different subjects. While I may not have known the subject matter, I enjoyed the planning and delivery. When my parents asked me what I wanted for Christmas, I would request things that enhanced my makeshift classroom i.e. chalkboard, paper, pencil and other items.

While I did not have a clue about gifts or specifically the gift of teaching, I was operating in it at a very young age. Throughout the journey, I started operating in other gifts. Or should I say they started operating in me without my knowledge. When I turned 14 years old, I started mobilizing my friends, writing short skits, directing, producing and teaching them. Still, I did not know I had other gifts. My parents did not understand the law of gifts; therefore, they were not able to recognize and hone in on it. Their focus was on raising us to be a doctors, lawyers and such! The least expected would be to become a nurse and make them proud. But here I was operating in something foreign to them. Something I did not know was changing me each day to become the person God intended for me to be.

Everyone has gifts, passion and purpose and if we pay close attention to the young people in our lives, we will see evidence of that at an early age.

This went on for years, but even at the age of 25, I still did not have a clue how to connect the dots. Did not even know what my true purpose was. I was a 25-year old woman, merely existing and not realizing how to make the connection. As a matter of fact, I did not realize there was a connection to be made. Furthermore, my relationship with God was not where it needed to be for me to come to any type of realization. I realize now that in discovering our gifts, a relationship with God must be the foundation.

I had accepted Christ as my Lord and Savior at the age of 22 but did not truly understand what that meant. I was still partying and hustling to make money. I started business after business, but still without knowing the truth. Going to Church on Sundays and leaving the same when service ended. All along I was missing something inside of me. I had come from a Catholic background; born and raised. My relationship with God had a middle man. If I did something wrong, I could go and ask the priest to ask God to forgive me. The priest would tell me to say some Hail Mary and Our Fathers, touch the Rosary and all would be well. I would get a fresh start to sin again, without real redemption.

It was not until I realized who I was in Christ, that I understood that God does speak to us about our purpose here on Earth. In Isaiah 40:31 God tells us, *"But those who hope in the LORD will renew their strength. They will soar on wings like eagles; they will run and not grow weary, they will walk and not be faint."*

Don't be discouraged about not knowing how to connect the dots or the fact that you don't feel connected yet. I say yet because if you woke up this morning and you are reading this sentence, this lets you know that there is still time. We have an opportunity to get it right each day. There is not a time schedule on when discovery comes. It's not a microwave situation and there are people in their 30's, 40's, 50's, 60's, 70's, and 80's who are still on the "JOURNEY BELT" and don't have a clue that they are there. There are people who die every day without knowing why they were here. Isn't it sad?

God loves you so much that He gave you spiritual gifts that you may live a life with purpose. We are to use all the gifts He has entrusted to us to bless and pour into His people.

It's as though your heavenly Father said, "Here my child, I trust you with these gifts." Sometimes we may not even realize that we have these gifts. When parents give a gift to their children and they don't see them use it, they may become frustrated and want to take it back. But not God. He has such a belief in us that one day we would use the gifts He has given to us. I often use this scenario- when you stand before God one day, will you still have your unused gifts in hand to return to him? I could see some people now "Well God, here is your gift back. I did not have time to use that one. Oh and here is another, I did not realize I had that one." We are supposed to use those gifts to help others. Your legacy should be that you died empty by giving God's people everything He entrusted to you. Dr. Myles Monroe said *"The wealthiest places in the world are not gold mines, oil fields, diamond mines or banks. The wealthiest place is the cemetery. There lie companies that were never started, masterpieces that were never painted… In the cemetery, there is buried the greatest treasure of untapped potential. There is a treasure within you that must come out. Don't go to the grave with your treasure still within YOU."*

I often say that Dr. Myles Monroe died empty in that plane crash on that Sunday evening of November 9, 2014. He left this earth empty of the gifts God gave to him because he spent every opportunity pouring them into others. His legacy will live on as a result of his obedience. What do you want said about you?

The other day, I was asked to write a resolution that would be read at a homegoing service for someone. It was difficult writing about this individual because there was not much recorded that I could say. They seemed to have spent most of their life raising their family and living in a sheltered world. Don't get me wrong, that is a good thing, but God calls us to do more. He is a God of the Nations, an International God. He is everywhere, and He cares about everything. It is imperative as my mentor Missionary Dr. Patricia Bailey often says, "We must have our thumb on the Pulse of God." This is significant because the pulse leads to the heart. Therefore, if our thumb is in place, we will know what God's concerns are. The good thing is that you can start living on purpose each day that you wake up. Start living for more than just yourself and your family and become concerned with what concerns our Father in Heaven.

My Journey to Purpose

> "Passion without knowing your gifts is purpose wasted"

> "All things God works for the good of those who love Him, who have been called according to His purpose" (Romans 8:28)

If I had read a book like this as a young woman growing up, it may have prevented me from going down some bumpy roads. While there were people in my life, like Dorothy of the National Council of Negro Women, who saw something in me, I did not see it in myself. As a teenager, I still did not understand purpose, God's purpose for my life. Due to not knowing my purpose, life at home forced me to look for love and companionship elsewhere. My dad was a successful businessman and well known in our community. He had migrated to the United States and he and my mother became very successful in the ownership of Corona Pest Control Company in Queens, New York. They later sent for my three brothers and me. I was five years old when I landed at John F. Kennedy International Airport in Jamaica, New York. My parents made sure we had everything we needed and was known as the wealthy family of the "hood!" My parents had the gift of giving. They gave to family, gave to friends and loved people all around. Our home was well kept, and we had the finest of things. However, there was a shadow that became evident. My father was an alcoholic. This affected our family tremendously. I remember dad drinking and he and mom would have these drawn-out arguments, which later turned into physical fights. They were so bad that I would sometimes try to stop the violence and ended up getting hurt myself. I still have one or two scars to prove it. I did not realize that God was stirring up passion in me even then. One day as I listened to a major argument happening in our store, a nightmare started to unfold. My mother was in the kitchen at the back of the store proceeding to put water on the stove intending to boil water for some rice (not sure if it was an intent). About 20 minutes later, in my father's drunken state, he went to the back room where my mother was and continued to argue with her. As I pleaded for them to stop, the splashes of hot boiling water grazed my arm. I tried to get out of the way as the water burned my skin. The screams of my father took my attention away from my small drops of hot water to my arm. I heard father scream out in pain again and muttered the words "What did you do to me?" I could see the thick wool sweater he was wearing on that cold winter night, smouldering with smoke. My mother had thrown the pot of hot water on my father's arms and chest. I started to scream as I watched my father try to get the sweater off his burning body. My middle brother, ran to get a pair of scissors and cut the sweater off my father. As he cut the sweater away, my father's skin peeled off with the sweater. My mom ran out to the car and left as the ambulance arrived to take my injured father to the hospital. He had second degree burns to his upper torso. Yes, through all of this, God was stirring my passion. The dots were connecting, but I did not see how and when.

At age 17, the violence continued in our home. Still not knowing gifts and my purpose, I met a young man in our neighborhood and started dating him without my parent's knowledge. They were too busy growing a business and fighting. He wowed me with his seemingly Jamaican charm, only to find out later that he wasn't even Jamaican. He made me promise after promise which he never kept. I was young and thought this was an escape from all the violence and quarrelling. Don't get me wrong! We had amazing family time and were devout Catholics that loved hard. But it was those dark times when things turned upside down.

I was searching for love from the Belizean young man, who I adored at this young age and didn't know what love was. One warm summer day, while my dad was asleep, recovering from a night of drinking and the alcoholic demon in full effect, my boyfriend talked me into coming over to his house. It was easy to communicate, because he lived right up the block, which was a short distance, in sight of our store. I can't remember what my mom was doing at that time, but she would normally have a good eye on me. She had become pregnant at that same age. When parents have experienced certain things, they tend to make sure their children don't experience that as well. That's called a "generational curse". She might have been trying to keep us away so we wouldn't wake my dad. The after-shock of an alcoholic argument is sometimes worse than the original fight. I could understand why she did not want to disturb his sobering sleep.

I watched the young man, who had my heart and my mind from a distance, as he made signals to me to come to his house. It was like a magnet, what I thought would be a state of calm and peace, drew me to his porch. I remember that day clearly. His mother, sister and friends were sitting outside when I approached. After a while, he invited me upstairs. To this day, I still don't understand why his mother allowed that foolishness. That day he talked me into having sex with him for the first time and something changed with my body. I became pregnant at seventeen with a blessing that others shunned me about. God was stirring up the gifts within me. Later in life, I had to share my story to help other young ladies experiencing teenage pregnancy. Today I mentor young girls facing the same challenges.

Not knowing my purpose and my worth was a key factor. Everyone turned their back on me. Including my mentor, whom I adored dearly. Some of my family and friends of my parents said I would be nothing. God was stirring my passion through the experience. I did not realize at the time that my story was for His glory! Today, my daughter is successful, beautiful and a jewel.

I went on to college two weeks after having my daughter to study pre-medicine. It was at the City College of New York when I started to discover my gifts and passions. My parents were not happy when I came home and told them during my second year of college that I wanted to become an actress and was changing my major. That's when I discovered my passion, but passion without knowing your gifts is purpose wasted.

The things I experienced was the catalyst in my starting to develop a heart for people. My emotions started to change. My heart made me watch what I said and did, always keeping people and their feelings in mind. Our hearts determine why we say the things we say and do the things we do. I had found what excites me, what appeals to me and something I truly care about. This thing gave me unspeakable joy.

And we know that in *all things God works for the good of those who love Him, who have been called according to His purpose" (Romans 8:28)*. Every experience, I had, the good, bad, ugly, indifferent, at work, in the family, in relationships inside and outside the church–blends to make us who we are. Even our past sins can be turned into purpose when we connect the dots.

It was at the age of 35, after the birth of our son Andrew, 19 years ago, when the dots started to connect for me. I went through another series of challenges in my marriage.

Through God using my husband to teach me how to forgive myself for past mistakes, the discovery of my gifts manifested themselves. I then realized that I have several gifts and more were to come. The dots started connecting in my life. My gift of teaching, helped me launch my first performing arts academy for children. My gift of discernment helped me see things spiritually and help people through the art of acting. My gift of hospitality and compassion has helped me develop my ministry group for women and teaching them. My gift of administration, helped me to produce plays, gospel concerts, conferences and much more for women. I soon realized that my purpose was people. To help others find their gifts, passions and live out their purpose through the arts and other avenues. Do you see how my dots were connecting?

He is the image of the invisible God, the firstborn over all creation. . .. For God was pleased to have all his fullness dwell in him. . .. But now he has reconciled you... .if you continue in your faith, established and firm, not moved from the hope held out in the gospel (Col. 1:15, 19, 22-23, NIV). He, in this scripture, is God's Son, Jesus.

This scripture gives hope to what we should be aspiring for as Christians. God loves us that much that He gave His only begotten Son that we may have life and have it more abundantly. He also gave us spiritual gifts. Jesus came to the earth in the form of man but was all of God and He was a gift to us. We must hold to our faith and hope in Him as we share our spiritual gifts with others. There is no one bigger than our God and only He could do what He did for mankind by imparting gifts into us. Jesus was touched with our infirmities and bruised for our iniquities. The chastisement of peace was upon His head and by His stripes, we are healed. He was crucified but left a comforter that now lives in us and helps us to live our purpose here on Earth.

CHAPTER 2

THERE ARE ENOUGH GIFTS FOR EVERYONE

S everal gifts are taught in the Bible. They are spoken of in Romans 12, 1 Corinthians 12 and 1 Peter 4. God has given everyone gifts through the working of the Holy Spirit.

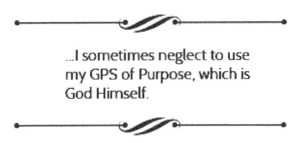

...I sometimes neglect to use
my GPS of Purpose, which is
God Himself.

Our Guide/Compass

> *"But I have raised you up for this very purpose,*
> *that I might show you my power and that my*
> *name might be proclaimed in all the earth"*
> *(Exodus 9:16).*

One day I was driving to an area I was not familiar with. I decided to use a GPS that my husband had given me as a gift! I am one of those people that don't like to use any apparatus or item when trying to figure things out. You know, the one who tries to put the bike together without reading or following the instructions that came in the box? That's me sometimes!

Well, I decided to start the GPS and headed to the destination. As I drove on the highway, I noticed that the voice was not providing me with the route I thought was best. I decided to shut off this talking box and figure out how to get there on my own, using this thing I thought I had called "Sense of Direction", you know it. Well, I got lost. I called myself trying to take a short cut. I started thinking of all the things my husband would say, especially "I told you so". Who wanted to hear that? I proceeded to turn this little box back on and allow it to help me on this journey as I tried to figure out where I was.

I pulled aside and turned the GPS back on and resumed the directions. To my surprise, the voice would not come on! I became a little frantic and thought talking to the box, would cause the sound to return, but to no avail! The sound would not return. The GPS had refused to talk to me because I felt I could do this on my own. Wow, it was at that moment I got some much-needed revelation. I sat there in the car, lost and trying to figure out what to do next. It made me think of my relationship with God! It dawned on me that I sometimes neglect to use my GPS of Purpose, which is God Himself. Sometimes we don't make the correlation that God is guiding us. We sometimes think that we can make it through this journey of life without Him and we turn Him off! With this, we are shutting Him out. That is a dangerous place to be. Sometimes I hear people say, "I can't hear from God". He has not left you. He is still there. Just like the GPS on your dashboard waiting to be activated and not ignored. In Exodus, we are reminded that we are here for His purpose alone *"But I have raised you up for this very purpose, that I might show you my power and that my name might be proclaimed in all the earth" (Exodus 9:16).*

When we turn off God (our spiritual GPS) we sometimes go through things that we do not have to! We need to learn not to be impatient, because God is not moving fast enough or at our pace. Just as I did when I shut off the GPS and tried to do it on my own, this is what happens when we feel we can make it through this journey on our own. We are made in His image and therefore like our children, God wants the best for us and will not lead us astray.

"Teach me Your way, O LORD, And lead me in a level path Because of my foes." Psalms 27:11

Another experience I had of not following the directions of my GPS, was om 2015. Yes, I said 2015. God is still working on me! All of us have sinned and fallen short of the glory of God! The songwriter said, "We fall down, but we get up". Last year, my Pastor T.J. McBride came to me and asked me to start a Global Missions Ministry, as the Lord had led Him. This involved creating a Missions Center and Missions Wall. I had never done anything of this magnitude, which involved creating a place where people can learn about the World and where we conduct missions work on each Continent.

Weeks went by and I could not figure out where to start in designing a Missions Wall. I then reached out to a graphics designer in our Church, who drew up a plan and preliminary design for me to review. He emailed me the design and when I opened it, my thought was, "What is this elementary sketch?" I think I said it out loud. I dismissed the design. Well, our grandchildren stayed over that night at our house. The very next morning when I went into our living room, I noticed our grandson had left his homework sitting on the couch. As I approached and looked at the paper, I could not believe what I saw. It was the same exact design sent to me by the graphics designer on the day before. Immediately negativity set in and I said to my husband and all who would listen, "You see, that sketch is elementary work." "We need something hi-tech and advanced." was what I babbled.

About one week later, while Pastor TJ was out of town, I was helping in our Christian Academy with a skit the children were getting ready to perform. I remember leaving the Church at about 11:00 am, got in my car and proceeded to leave the parking lot. It was then I heard a still voice, that sound like it was someone sitting right next to me. What astonished me, was not that I heard the voice, but the fact that the voice spoke to me. I heard "Go to the church Chris" before I could think about it, I answered saying "What church? I am at the church." I proceeded to the light and there was the voice again, right next to me saying "Go to the Church Chris!" and again I answered, "What church?" I approached the stoplight, which was red, leaving the parking lot and the voice answered me and said, "Just drive, I will lead you." I knew that my God, GPS system, was activated, but was confused. I said to the voice, "I am supposed to make a left here and go home." The voice told me to go straight ahead. I knew there was a church on that road but just did not think about it at the moment. As I approached the turning lane into the Church, the voice said, "Turn in here. This is the church". As I turned into this parking lot, which was less than a mile from my church, I was moved by the magnitude of the size of the campus. I proceeded to drive towards the beautiful edifice, and low and behold, I looked up at the massive glass window. To my surprise what I saw next was jaw-dropping! There it was; a wall four times the size of the wall intended for Global Missions at our Church with the same sketch that had been given to me twice. Once, when the graphics artist sent it to me in an email and then again my grandson's homework.

God had been my GPS twice and I ignored or doubted what he had sent for me. I figured God was telling me that He gave me what I needed through the graphics artist and I doubted by finding the negative in it. "I gave you what you needed, by having your grandson's homework, laid out before your eyes at the crack of dawn, yet you still doubted. Well, here it is larger than life." I felt He was saying. He had to show it to me magnified before I would get it.

I immediately went to the office of that Church and asked the secretary to let me inside the church. The woman heard the urgency in my voice and stopped what she was doing, got the key and went across the parking lot to open the door for me. She explained everything I needed to know and then some. You can imagine my ride home. The good thing is that the Holy Spirit never says, "I told you so"! That experience never ceases to amaze me.

I recently took a closer look at my GPS and paralleled it to how God helps us to navigate to our purpose and plans He has for us. The GPS gives us choices of where we want and need to go. We just have to turn it on and enter our choices. Well, just like the GPS, God allows us choices and when we activate his navigation in our life, He will guide us on a straight path. A path that is best for reaching our destination of purpose.

Embrace your own gifts and celebrate the gifts of Others

These experiences I have shared with you are just a few of those that help me realize and know that God is my GPS/Navigation system and He can and will guide me through anything. It is up to you to turn Him on in your life. We turn the Navigation on for God to guide us, by reading his word daily, praising and worshipping Him and asking Him to lead you to your purpose here on Earth. The sooner you realize that you can't take this journey without Him, the sooner you will be able to connect the dots. That's where it begins.

I remember the lines in the gym at my high school back in Forest Hills, Queens, when we would register for classes back in the day. There were tables, with signs that displayed the classes available and we would have to go to that table and register for those classes. I often relate that experience to how we obtained our spiritual gifts and talents. When God was giving us our gifts, it may have been the same type of set up. I sometimes envision myself in that same setting and I saw a talent line that said "singing", well I think I did not go to that line but planned on returning later. Needless to say, I did not get back to that line, because I can't hold a note. The good thing about it is He still loves me enough that He blessed me with an ear for "good singing." I have a love for music and an appreciation for beautiful music. While we may not have some gifts we wish we had, He still made sure we each left the registration table with something. It is important that we *embrace our own gifts and celebrate the gifts of others.* People tend to laugh whenever I say to them, "I have a song on my heart, please sing it." They would sometimes say, "Well if it's on your heart, then maybe you should sing it." I knew if I did, they would clear the room immediately. Those close to me, now understand. I don't know if the choir members at my church realize how much they bless me. I make it a point to tell them every opportunity I get.

The main root to not seeing and being able to experience our gifts is jealousy. *Love is patient, love is kind. It does not envy, it does not boast, it is not proud. 1 Corinthians 13:4.* It's important to remember that jealousy is not a gift from God, but a sin that is not of God. Some people spend time being jealous of the gift of others that they miss out on their gifts. You are special to God and He loves you just as He loves anyone else. God is no respecter of persons and loves us all the same. Yes, you heard me, He loves the person you sometimes can't stand to be in the same room with. He loves us unconditionally. No matter what you did last year, yesterday or just a few minutes ago. He is just to forgive you of your sins and still entrust you with His gifts. If there is jealousy in your heart or you are not sure, stop right where you are and say these words before moving to the next chapter in this book.

> *Father God in Heaven*
> *Forgive me for being Jealous of others (or name the person)*
> *Clean my heart of this Jealousy*
> *Help me to walk in my calling and discover my spiritual gifts and purpose*
> *In Jesus' Name*
> *Amen!*

CHAPTER 3

WHAT ARE THE GIFTS
MENTIONED IN ROMANS

I was nineteen years old and still in college when I discovered I had the gift of teaching. I heard there was an opening for an Adjunct Teacher in Bushwick, Brooklyn. Bushwick was an area with a reputation for being unsafe. My husband and I were living in Crown Heights, Brooklyn and to get to Bushwick, required taking two buses which was over an hour in travel time. We decided that I would go for the interview because the money was attractive. The salary was about $18,000 annually and that was a good sum of money back in those days. After a long ride to Bushwick, I entered the building that was once a Catholic School. The main office was two flights up. The receptionist was a medium built woman with long hair and in her fifties. She spoke with a heavy Latin accent. I later realized that she was Puerto Rican. She was sort of stern but treated me with respect. She looked at me with eyes that said "You are too young for this job". She gave me an application to complete and after finishing, a short man approached from the hallway and said "Hi, I am Mr. Herman." Mr. Herman was a devout Jew, originally from Florida, with a cul-de-sac or receding hairline. He had a warm smile and a welcoming posture. He led me to a classroom with about ten students. These students were about two years younger than I was. I later found out that one young lady was older than me. The students had lots of questions for me that day. I later realized that *was* my interview. A few days later, I received a phone call from Mr. Herman offering me the job. That became my second teaching job. I failed to mention to you that my first teaching job was as a typing instructor for a place call Cashier Training Institute in New York City. The job at the Youth Center with Mr. Herman made me realize, although I did not know at the time, my gift of teaching. There it was all along, being developed and I did not have a clue that it was precious.

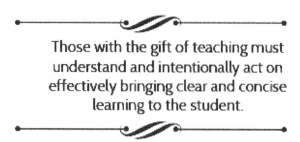

Those with the gift of teaching must understand and intentionally act on effectively bringing clear and concise learning to the student.

Let's take a look at teaching first. I recently read a book by Bruce Wilkinson, entitled "The Seven Laws of the Learner", which helped shed light on the gift of teaching. This book speaks about the seven Retention Maxims that must be explored. Wilkinson's writing caused me to take a closer look at this gift which I also possess. Those that have the gift of teaching must realize that it is their responsibility that the student retains the information learned. Many teachers battle with this over and over. I have heard teachers say time and time again that it's not their fault if the student can't remember things taught to them. I feel that this is a selfish way for those with the gift of teaching to think, or do they have the gift of teaching at all? The person with the gift of teaching must find ways to evaluate if the student effectively understands what was taught or is being taught.

The person with the gift of teaching can relate the content to real-life situations. A teacher must be able to relate the content to real-life situations. When connections to everyday situations are made, retention of the information becomes more relevant to the learner.

My son recently told his dad and I that he wants to become an actor. This was very surprising to both of us because we just knew he was Navy bound. After four years in NJROTC we just never thought of him doing anything else. Well, he came to me and asked me to teach him acting. This was very difficult for me to do. I have used my gift of teaching as an acting coach for many years, but when it came to teaching my son, it was not as enjoyable as teaching has always been for me. For a moment, it made me question my gift of teaching. I wondered if I had lost it because I could not find the patience to teach my teenager. I had to pray and ask God to help me find a way to give Andrew all that I have given many students over thirty years. Well, God granted me the patience I prayed for and I soon realized that my gift was still in place, but the student was different.

Those with the gift of teaching must understand and intentionally act on effectively bringing clear and concise learning to the student. While this may not have seemed to be the issue in teaching Andrew, it helps me to improve my method with his style of learning.

The method of illustration seems to be the most effective and is also key in utilizing the gift of teaching. There is power in communicating information through show-and-tell. People learn in various ways, but illustrations have proven to be the most effective in my experience.

I can recall when my Pastor used the illustration to teach on tithing. He utilizes it as a way of summing things up. One Sunday, he illustrated tithing by placing two tables on the pulpit, having a large basket of fruit, filled with ten of each type. He used one table to represent what God commands that we give (10 percent, one fruit) and the other table with what God says we may keep (90 percent, 9 fruit). The table with the larger percentage of fruit was overflowing onto the pulpit and people were responding with shouts, hallelujahs and thank you, Jesus! This illustration helped confirm that people are more impacted by seeing rather than just hearing and that's why it allows for lessons to be more effective in communicating. What my Pastor did with his gift of teaching, was to use one of the most valuable methods of teaching.

> *There are different kinds of gifts, but the same Spirit distributes them. 1 Corinthians 12:4*

Spiritual Gifts

In the next two chapters, we will take a look at some of the gifts listed in the Bible. My hope in writing this book is that with the help of your Godly GPS system, you will be able to discover or confirm your gifts and begin to operate in them.

The Gift of Administration

The gift of administration is a powerful spiritual gift that helps in many ways. It's the divine strength or ability to organize multiple tasks and groups of people to accomplish these tasks. As I write, a good friend and sister in Christ comes to mind and a smile came upon my face. She has the gift of administration like nothing I have ever experienced before. I have had secretaries in my secular jobs as well as administrative assistants and she has outshined them all. Her way of operating gives me a clearer understanding of the gift of administration. When you heard the word administration, you probably thought about paperwork and deskwork, right? It's way beyond those things. Persons with this gift are talented, organized, able to do many things at one time and are strong leaders. My friend is my right hand in the Global Missions Ministry at my Church. I would later introduce her as the person who handles all the administrative things as well as passports. She once pulled me to the side and said, "I think I do more than just handle passports." We both laughed, and I realized she was right. The gift of administration on her life has helped to build an organization within our church that has raised up and deployed Missionaries to Haiti, Dominican Republic, Jamaica and Belize. She is a processor; well organized, can multi-task, loves people and leads them to success. The gift of administration is easy to recognize. Take time and think of someone in your life or even yourself and assess if you or them may have this gift. Those who possess this gift are also planners. They see the full picture and usually make excellent event planners. The book of Luke tells us the importance of planning. Someone once said, *"if you fail to plan, you plan to fail."*

> *"Suppose one of you wants to build a tower. Won't you first sit down and estimate the cost to see if you have enough money to complete it? For if you lay the foundation and are not able to finish it, everyone who sees it will ridicule you, saying, 'This person began to build and wasn't able to finish."*
> *LUKE 14:28 -30 (NIV)*

My gift of administration was predominantly in operation when I worked for a company called PSI. It is an organization with such core values as Integrity, Trustworthy and Customer Satisfaction. Based in Denver, Colorado, they were known to treat their employees with dignity and respect. With these in mind, it was imperative to ensure that every area of Human Resources was covered, which involved having the gift of administration or should I say a double portion of it. The company provided support to companies and government agencies with quality program development in the health and human services industry.

The need for Human Resources and Management to work together was important in providing for a successful new site. PSI was contracted to provide consulting services in process redesign, child support services, employment and training, government healthcare, health and human services, justice, systems development and much more. What was I to do with this major task at hand? My gift of administration had to be stirred up or was it already in operation?

This gift gave me the skills to develop a comprehensive written document outlining policy and procedures for the new location. I was able to develop this document with the management team.

When we first opened the location, most of the managers were new hires and had never worked for PSI in the past. This required an extensive management training program from the Human Resources Department. I was chosen to staff this project due to the powerful gift operating in me. It was somewhat difficult, because we were not a fully functioning department yet. I was a generalist and did not have access to the necessary resources that it would take to provide full support and training to these new managers, but the Holy Spirit provided all that was needed.

Philippians 4:19 But my God shall supply all your need according to his riches in glory by Christ Jesus.

If you have been graced with the gift of administration, it is important to be consistent. In my position as a Human Resources manager, I was able to help the company function effectively by being consistent in operation and ensuring equality to prevent lawsuits against the company. The gift of administration will allow you to manage and juggle several things at one time; be a multi-tasker. People always say things to me like "you are doing too much", "where do you get time to do all that you do?" and many other odd things. It's just that they may not be operating in the gift of administration. They clearly don't understand.

In the Human Resources position at another company, my gift of administration was in full effect. I managed four areas of human resources. The first was Recruiting and Staffing. I worked with the management team to identify the current needs of the company for our location, create requisitions and determined the most effective means of filling those requisitions. There came a need to hire a recruitment staff, due to the intensive growth of the call center and it all became a little too much for one person with the gift of administration.

The second area was Benefits, within the HR department. This section was responsible for acquiring and managing employee benefits, such as health, vision dental insurance, 401K plans, retirement funds, non-cash payouts and such.

Employee Relations was my favorite component of the Human Resources Department. This section helped to maintain a high level of employee satisfaction. Employee relations involved several incentive programs and other creative ways that helped to boost morale and impact retention positively. It was helping me to grow in my gift of administration. Are you seeing this gift in you?

Training and Development go hand in hand, as it helps develop a strong team of employees as well as managers. I created a curriculum for training our new hires and managers to ensure growth and prevent legal ramifications. Sexual harassment was one of the key training curriculums to Policy Studies Incorporated. As you read further, you will see that my gift of teaching was also being used at this company. I had the opportunity to use another gift here.

The Gift of Discernment

I believe we all have been blessed with the gift of discernment. Some people think it is intuition. However, I believe that it's more than that. You too have the gift; it just hasn't been activated. Merriam-Webster dictionary defines discernment as the quality of being able to grasp and comprehend what is obscure: skill in discerning. I don't know about you, but this definition sounds spiritual to me.

The Biblical meaning of discernment is the divine strength or ability to spiritually identify falsehood, to distinguish between right and wrong motives and the spiritual forces at work in situations. We sometimes give credit to intuition and our minds. Have you ever wondered or asked yourself, "How do I know the Holy Spirit is talking to me?" Have you ever been in your car or a situation where a still voice tells you, "Don't go that way; go this way." That is the gift of discernment trying to operate in you. Have you ever had a funny feeling about something or someone that just did not seem right? Discernment can also make you feel good about something right. It's good to help your children discover the gift of discernment at a young age. It would help them make better decisions in life. Through prayer and worship, discernment is strengthened within you. Communicating with God daily is key in being effective in this gift or better yet, it being effective in you.

The Gift of Evangelism

The gift of evangelism can be misunderstood by others at times. Evangelism is the divine strength or ability to help non-Christians take the necessary steps to become a born-again Christian. I remember growing up in New York City in the Catholic faith. We were reserved and quietly worshipped God. I was not used to loud shouting and sudden outbursts in church or anywhere else as a matter of fact. The experiences with evangelism at that time were different. There would be a few on street corners shouting things like "Repent, for the Kingdom of God is at hand!" or

"You will go to hell if you don't repent this day!" Some walk through the train cars shouting messages with urgency. Most people would ignore them. No one would tell them to be quiet or go somewhere else. They would just let them speak their message. In our minds, we would think that they were "crazy", because of the outbursts. It was not until I found Christ for myself that I discovered that an evangelist had a passion for saving souls for the Kingdom of God! The person with the gift of evangelism is passionate about winning souls and are 'fishers of men'. Some may be like those on the train, shouting the message loud, while others may be soft in their manner. Evangelism is a special gift. Not everyone delivers the message in the same way. Recently, during a Missions trip to the Dominican Republic, one of our Missionaries taught us never to leave home without our 'fishing rod'. As a result, the phrase "leave no stone unturned" was developed for the team. These two phrases simply mean to be always ready to lead someone to Christ. I believe it was the last day of the trip when the Pastor took us to a beautiful flowing river. Here the water was crystal clear and drinkable. We waded in the water and it felt like a baptism was taking place. It was an amazing time of fellowship with the other missionaries. The various rocks, waterfall and nicely carved mountainside was clear evidence that only God's Hands could have created such a masterpiece. As we climbed back up the short mountain and walked past the same seven young men we saw on the way down the mountain, something suddenly transformed into our actual purpose of being there. Although we went with a feeling that this was a moment for us to relax and hear from God for ourselves, God allowed the gift of evangelism to come forth in the missionary's life. She stopped us all in our tracks as she turned back and spoke to the seven young men, who were clothed in urban wear, with chains that held crosses on them. The sad thing is that we did not recognize that these were souls waiting to be won for the Kingdom and almost missed the mark. Thank God for the one missionary amongst us that had the gift of evangelism operating. Not saying that others present did not have it, but it was prevalent in her. After telling them about Jesus Christ, she asked them to repeat the "sinners confession" after her. She then immediately had us form a circle, holding hands with the seven men and prayed for them. These young men gave their lives to the Lord on that riverbank in the Dominican Republic that beautiful day in October 2017. Think about it. God could have chosen someone right there in the country to lead these men to Christ, but He chose us. We took a flight, drove miles and ended up there at the river that day for God to use us through this vessel's gift of evangelism. Do you have a passion for lost souls? Does it affect you when you think of where someone might spend eternity? Do you have a desire to lead someone to Christ? Then you may have the gift of Evangelism.

The Gift of Giving

> Deuteronomy 28:1-2 "Now it shall come to pass, if you diligently obey the voice of the LORD your God, to observe carefully all His commandments which I command you today, that the LORD your God will set you high above all nations of the earth. And all these blessings shall come upon you and overtake you because you obey the voice of the LORD your God."

Have you ever wonder why some unsaved people are still being financially blessed? Take a look at Bill Gates, one of the wealthiest men in the world. I really can't say if he is saved or not, but he, like many others have the gift of giving. As for Christians, the Gift of Giving must put seeking God first! The gift of giving has to be activated by just doing it and looking for nothing in return. It's directly connected to the Biblical concept of reaping and sowing. When giving you should give freely to others, be cheerful about it and not expect anything back. It's that simple! Let's take a look at the gift of giving and how it relates to Biblical Prosperity.

The success of giving can be measured and evident as seen in Biblical Prosperity.

Some people measure success and prosperity in different ways. The gift of giving is key for Christians. To truly achieve Biblical Prosperity, we must diligently seek after God in everything that we do. The scripture tells us in Matthew 6:33 where we are given a clear directive to prosperity "But seek ye first the kingdom of God, and his righteousness, and all these things shall be added unto you". This means that we should not run after material things, but run after God.

Some people spend a lifetime chasing a dream and yet forget who sits high and looks low when they are being blessed as a result of the gift of giving. They wonder why they feel like an animal that is chasing their tail and not getting anywhere with a lack of true joy. In seeking God, we must pursue His righteousness. To pursue His righteousness means to live the way He wants us to live and use our gift of giving. A keen sense of discernment is necessary to utilize this gift correctly.

We must follow Him and be Godly examples of God here on Earth, as He gave to us first. God gave the ultimate gift, for us to have life and have it more abundantly. This is a spiritual gift we should all have. It is important to live according to the fruit of the spirit, as in Galatians 5:22-23, But the fruit of the Spirit is love, joy, peace, forbearance, kindness, goodness, faithfulness, gentleness and self-control. Against such things, there is no law. The fruit of the Spirit is also a form in which we should give to others.

The gift of giving is also directly connected to keep the commandments of God. We cannot expect God to bless us when we do not strive to bless others. The best example that comes to mind for me is when our oldest daughter went away to college. The stipulations that my husband and I gave were she had to follow certain rules while away from home. If these simple rules were not followed she would not be provided with the type of financial support she needed while away from home, which included sowing and sending tithes to the home church. I think of God in that sense. We cannot expect our Heavenly Father to bless us with earthly goods if we are not following His rules (commandments). We are reminded of the importance of God's commandments in Deuteronomy 28:1-2 "Now it shall come to pass, if you diligently obey the voice of the LORD your God, to observe carefully all His commandments which I command you today, that the LORD your God will set you high above all nations of the earth. And all these blessings shall come upon you and overtake you because you obey the voice of the LORD your God."

The other key to the gift of giving is to give to others and honor God with our finances. I always use this statement to others, "When you take care of God's house and His people, He will take care of your house". We must make it a lifestyle to help others, pay our tithes and offering. We must realize that giving is a form of worship to God. When we give, we are honoring our Heavenly Father. God does not say we must give all our money, which belongs to Him anyway.

Dr. Bill Winston mentions that we are a member of the NFL, National Faith League and we must have faith in our giving. This is another key to activating the gift of giving and will lead us to how God has intended for us to live. The Bible instructs us on faith in Hebrews 11:1, "Now faith is the substance of things hoped for, the evidence of things not seen". We know that without Faith, it is impossible to please God. Sometimes it is difficult to believe in the things we don't see, but in order to achieve, we must trust in God and not lean on our understanding. These keys will lead you to maximize the gift of giving within.

Do you feel you have one or more of the gifts mentioned in this chapter of this book? Maybe you are starting to **connect the dots to your purpose**.

In the next chapter, we will explore a few more gifts. If you don't see any of these gifts operating in you, just hold on, because something will leap on the inside of you when discovery comes. I promise!

The Gift of Encouragement

Sometimes I wonder why God entrusted me with such an amazing gift. This spiritual gift operates in me and I have learned to operate in it. The gift of encouragement or exhortation is found in Paul's list of gifts in Romans 12:7–8. The word translated "encouragement" or "exhortation" is the Greek word paraklésis, related to the word paraclete. Paraklésis means "a call to one's side."

If you have the spiritual gift of encouragement you can use it in both public and private settings. Encouragement is useful in counseling, discipleship, mentoring, and preaching. The body of Christ is built up in faith as a result of the ministry of those with the gift of encouragement. As a Ministry Consultant at my Church, this gift is extremely important. Ministry Consultants help others to find their spiritual gifts.

The gift of encouragement or exhortation differs from the gift of teaching. Exhortation focuses on the practical application of the Bible, whereas one with the gift of teaching focuses on the meaning and content of the Word, and one with the gift of encouragement focuses on the practical application of the Word. With this gift, you can relate to others, in groups and individually, with understanding, sympathy, and positive guidance. Teaching tells you how to do it; encouragement says, you can do it. If you have this spiritual gift you can help another person move from pessimism to optimism.

I have administered and completed Spiritual Gifts Assessments over a ten-year period. My most valuable spiritual gift is encouragement, listed in the Bible as exhortation is found in Paul's list of gifts in Romans 12:7-8. My gift of encouragement and exhortation is my key reason for the first value of NURTURING. My love and concern for people help facilitate a positive atmosphere. In my positions as volunteer coordinator, volunteer supervisor or volunteer director, those who work with me have been positively affected and enjoy serving and helping others, which I believe to be directly related to the gift of encouragement operating in me. I have gained their TRUST and foster encouragement for their own goals and aspirations. I ask my volunteers about their jobs, families and careers. This shows that I truly care about each of them and their success overall. My love and passion to see people succeed are rooted in my success. The volunteers I have and continue to work with have bought into my vision and whatever project I engage them to assist in. The trust factor has been established. I know that my ability to make people feel a sense of belonging and value is immeasurable and not to be taken for granted.

There are many ways in which I have used my gift of encouragement to help others and you can do the same. Goal-setting, training, and experience sharing have all been important in me growing and developing a strong team. This is fostered by my COMMITMENT to them. My volunteers know that I value them and God has entrusted them into my care. Throughout the year, I meet with my volunteers in group settings to set goals, by having them create a vision board to encompass, not only the work with me, but personally. This is the gift of encouragement at its best. The vision board concept helps them to stay on track and ensure a strong finish at the end of the year. I also train and re-train the volunteers on customer service skills and the importance of effective communication in interaction with the community. In these sessions, I encourage the volunteers to speak openly and share experiences they have encountered in volunteering; whether good or bad. I have found that sharing their experience is two-fold because the volunteers can release any frustrations from non-desirable experiences as well as share best practices that help others in the room.

There are times, when I find it necessary to revisit the matching of skillset to volunteers and I don't mind, because the gift of encouragement is operating in me, just as it will in you. Sometimes my volunteers may have been earmarked for a certain department of assignment and together we may make the determination to reassign the individual, possibly retake a gifts assessment or their desires may have been redirected. I also use techniques to assist the volunteer in re-identifying their skillset and interest. I have learned that interest and skillset can change over a period, due to life experiences. Those working with me can see my value of LOYALTY.

I have implemented a process in my position as a volunteer coordinator which includes, what I call "post-production" follow-up. This session has proven to be of equal importance as planning the volunteerism segment. I designed this segment to close the loop on an event by determining what worked, what did not work and areas of improvement. I have incorporated soliciting ideas from volunteers on the project completed, discuss events and questions and answers. The question and answers component adds value to the volunteers and enables them to be key contributors to the success of the event. This also helps to foster an environment of involvement, because I answer questions they may have, and I impart my value of OPTIMISM when things don't go as expected.

It is important that any organization or business that wants to be successful to implement teams to help develop and manage core values, for employees to model. This stands true for churches and ministries as well. All churches should have a Mission and Vision Statement that includes their values. Members will seek to include those values in their everyday life.

Over my 30 years of working as a volunteer coordinator or supervisor in various organizations, I have learned the importance of involving volunteers, because they bring necessary skills, save money, increase community awareness and involvement and fresh new energy to a project. The training of volunteers to help recruit other volunteers is successful in my position. The most phenomenal outcome for me is the joy and increase in the number of volunteers from word of mouth. Due to the satisfaction and appreciation I show my volunteers, they encourage others to be a part of my team. I have implemented a volunteer recognition program at Tabernacle of Praise Church International and the Caribbean Association of Georgia Inc. in which the very foundation is the core values of commitment, loyalty, optimism, nurturing and trust. I host a ceremony each year to recognize each of my volunteers by using my gift of encouragement to uplift others. This provides the volunteer with a sense of pride and builds their yearning to want to stay on my team. Using your gift of encouragement is the best form of volunteer recruiting and growth. Core Values must be the base of any organization that involves service.

For many years, I did not realize how passionate I was about people and my desire to see them succeed. You see, if you have a passion for people, you have the gift of encouragement operating in you. Do you celebrate for others when something good happens for them? Do you want to shout from the top of a mountain when God blesses them? I remember when I took a class called "Purpose Driven Life", by Rick Warren when we lived in Florida. This class helped me to discover my purpose and passion for people. I realized that God gave me an extra amount of love for other people. Back then things used to affect me differently. This thing we call "church hurt", seemed to be lurking. I used to be concerned with who liked me and who did not like me, therefore my heart was susceptible to pain. This usually occurs when you have the gift of encouragement.

It's not until we later moved to Georgia and I was working in the office of my church and one day my pastor said to me:

"Chris because of your passion for people, it's the area you will be hurt in the most!"

Although it hurt to hear him say that and a little bit of fear may have set in, it was the beginning of something new for me. It was then that God gave me my favorite scripture and I started to meditate on it day and night. It is Psalm 119:165 (KJV) *Great peace have they which love thy law: and nothing shall offend them.*

This scripture verse has helped me through *people hurt* many times over. You see God will give you what you need to effectively operate in the gifts He has entrusted to you. We must realize that we do not fight against people, but what's fighting against them.

Ephesians 6:12 *For we are not fighting against flesh-and-blood enemies, but against evil rulers and authorities of the unseen world, against mighty powers in this dark world, and against evil spirits in the heavenly places.*

If you have the gift of encouragement, you are beginning to "connect the dots to your purpose." Keep on helping and encouraging others. You may have said many times over, "I am done, I am not helping or encouraging another person, they don't appreciate me." After all the whining, you got yourself together and started all over again. You can't help yourself but encourage others. It's your God-given gift!

> *Proverbs 27:17 (NIV) As iron sharpens iron, so one person sharpens another.*

This scripture is important to those operating in the gift of encouragement. It's necessary to surround yourself with people that will pour encouragement right back into you. To pour something into others, you must have something in you. We can get tired and worn down by the giving of ourselves and must be replenished.

There is a good friend of mine that I serve with in ministry. I can always count on her pouring back into me. She is what I call "consistent". Whenever she calls me, or I call her, she encourages my heart. She would say "good morning FAM". I soon found out that FAM is short for "fearless amazing mentor". No matter what I am feeling, she will still say it and it would bring a smile to my face.

Think of the people in your life and what role they play. Are they sharpening you? If you can't think of anyone who helps sharpen you, then pray and ask God to surround you with those that will pour into you and help replenish you for serving others.

CHAPTER 4

THE SPIRITUAL GIFTS OF THE SHEPHERD

If you have one of the gifts of shepherding, you will notice that you are drawn to visible leadership as a person of influence. This chapter will give you some insight into the traits and characteristics of the persons with this gift category.

While the words *servant* and *leader* seem opposite, they mirror one another. It is important to first learn how to serve others to become an effective leader. For years I could not figure out why I get such pleasure in helping and serving others. I would be the one to attend a party but want to help serve the food or something else to help brings a smile to faces. These attributes are a sign of servanthood. The ultimate display of servanthood was Jesus washing the feet of others. To be a servant means being the hands and feet of God.

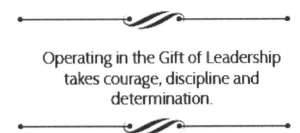

Operating in the Gift of Leadership takes courage, discipline and determination.

The gift of Leadership

Exodus 18:21 (ESV)

21 Moreover, look for able men from all the people, men who fear God, who are trustworthy and hate a bribe, and place such men over the people as chiefs of thousands, of hundreds, of fifties, and of tens.

The gift of leadership is also a valuable spiritual gift. Remember I told you in a previous chapter that we have gifts that sit dormant until they are activated? Well, sometimes we are operating in the gift and don't even know it.

The gift of leadership is one of the gifts God has entrusted me with and when I would gather the children in my neighborhood to join me for church in my parents' basement or to perform a play, this gift was activated in me. The missing link was I did not even know it! What was this desire to lead people to do things they never thought about doing? I would ask them to come and they would not question why. While the gift of leadership is good, it must be coupled with the law of leadership.

When I was in Ministry School, my Pastor gave us an assignment to read a book by John Maxwell called the "21 Irrefutable Laws of Leadership". This book helped solidify my gift of leadership in many ways. People often found it amazing that folks would just show up because I asked them to be at a certain place at a certain time. They would not ask any questions. When the leader of the event would ask most of them "who invited you and why did you come?" Most would say "Because Chris Scott asked me to come." That's when I connected the dots of my gift of leadership and the law of influence as noted in Maxwell's book.

Operating in the gift of leadership takes courage, discipline and determination. Leadership most times comes at the cost of you being unfairly judged by others. There are many leaders mentioned in the Bible and we can read how God has blessed them for their dedication. Several men and women in the Bible stepped up to the plate and became wonderful leaders. However, like most leaders, many did not want to be leaders, but the gift was making them restless. I asked someone the other day at my church to sit up front with me. She said, "Oh no, I am good with sitting in the back." I know this person has the gift of leadership stirring within her, but she is afraid of what people may think of her. Keep in mind that leadership is not management and does not require offending others to operate effectively in this gift.

The gift of leadership means that you have sufficient capacity to lead others in any situation. Do you have the gift of leadership? Did something leap in you as you read the last paragraph?

Let's explore John Maxwell's Law of Leadership and influence as it pertains to the law of influence.[2] The way Maxwell explains the Law of Influence is quite compelling. It is amazing that a leader cannot be pointed out from a group of people based on looks. This point made me remember a visit to a movie studio in Conyers, Georgia. I was sitting at the desk with the Administrative Assistant when this man entered the office. He was short in stature, wore jeans and sneakers and looked like any ordinary Joe on the street, but there was something different about him. He did not say much, but his presence gave me the sense that he was someone to be reckoned with. When he spoke introducing himself to me, he never mentioned that he was the owner and executive director of the studio. He simply said his name. It was not until he left, I was informed that he was the owner and executive director of the mega studio. Looks do not define a leader!

Although we cannot tell by looking at a person if he/she is a leader, I believe that a strong leader exudes some type of confidence that shines in their walk, talk and movements. Influence is a major factor in being a good leader. The Law of Influence is demonstrated to its fullest in the movie, Malcolm X, which I enjoy watching time and again. The most powerful scene in the movie was when a large group of men were very angry. With one wave of his hand, Malcolm X commanded the men to be silent and you could have heard a pin drop. Every man became quiet and stood at the attention of a leader. The police chief was astonished, and his words were simple, but memorable, when he said, "that is too much power for one man to have". That was his gift of leadership coupled with The Law of influence operating at fullest capacity.

Maxwell's book tells us of five myths about leadership that we need to examine in order to evaluate ourselves as leaders. The Management Myth is a huge misconception of leadership. Managers are usually employees in charge of other employees. Due to laws governed by the EEOC and other government employment organizations, they are to follow certain guidelines to keep people in a systematic concept. This is not leadership, but merely the act of getting people to do what you need them to do for a paycheck in return.

The second is the Entrepreneur Myth. I personally know of business owners that can neither manage nor lead someone else. There are awesome business owners, pastors, teachers and supervisors that just don't have the people skills necessary to be a good leader. To be a good leader, you must "like" people.

Then we have The Knowledge Myth. I think of this myth as being the same as the best surgeon in the world and cannot teach the art of surgery. The person may be full of information/knowledge about a particular subject but cannot communicate/transfer that same information to someone else.

The Pioneer Myth is another misconception of being a leader. There are people I call starters. They may be able to see a project from the beginning to a certain point. However, they cannot carry it to its fullest capacity. The starter/creator of a project is not always the leader, however, may have the gift of Apostleship (mentioned in the Appendix).

Lastly in Maxwell's Law of Influence, is The Position Myth. This happens often in the practice of Nepotism. Family-owned businesses usually experience failure through this misconception, because they hire members for positions in which they do not have the qualifications to fill. The higher the position does not mean the stronger the leader. Let's make the position and not expect the position to make us.

If you have the gift of leadership, it's important to be careful with placing family members in positions when they don't qualify.

The Son of Man did not come to be served, but to serve." (Matt. 20:28)

Most importantly, those with the gift of leadership must learn how to first be a servant. There has never been another leader that has walked this Earth greater than Jesus, yet He was a servant! We must not abuse this gift, because we could lead people down the wrong road. That's why when a church experiences the fall of a pastor, people don't know what to do, because in most cases they were following man and not God. It's necessary to let people know to follow Christ and not you!

Servanthood is necessary for becoming an effective leader. There are good leaders and there are great leaders. If leadership is your gift, are you good or great? It's alright if you said good because there is still time to become better. But "hurry!"

Your attitude is one of the most important parts of being a leader. We should not esteem ourselves higher than those we lead. If you are a great leader, they will treat you as such. You won't have to demand respect, it will just be inevitable.

Who, being in very nature God, did not consider equality with God something to be grasped, but made himself nothing, taking the very nature of a servant, being made in human likeness. And being found in appearance as a man, he humbled himself and became obedient to death--even death on a cross! (Phil. 2:5-8)

We must follow the life of Christ to obtain a clear example of servanthood because servanthood is a lifestyle and not a one-time thing. God rewards servanthood and we also feel a sense of satisfaction from helping others. Last year our organization volunteered at the USO at Hartsfield Jackson International Airport. We provided meals and served many soldiers and their families that day as we have done for the past seven years. The smiles and acts of gratitude from those we served gave us a feeling of accomplishment and satisfaction. These feelings in themselves are rewards from God.

There are ten characteristics of the servant leader of critical importance mentioned by Larry C. Spears,[3] however, there are a few more I will address here. The writer lists:listening, empathy, healing, awareness, persuasion, conceptualization, foresight, stewardship, commitment to the growth of people, and building community. Empathy and compassion are synonymous in this instance.

Some dictionaries would say that empathy is the action of understanding, being aware of, being sensitive to, and vicariously experiencing the feelings, thoughts, and experience of another of either the past or present without having the feelings, thoughts, and experience fully communicated in an objectively explicit manner. These are two key traits to possess a servant's heart. (Merriam-Webster Dictionary)

True servanthood and leadership require Godly work ethics. The Bible tells us not to be lazy or it could lead to failure. It's important to find satisfaction in serving others. Those who have the gift of servanthood will always be lead to volunteering, serving and giving to others. The principle of serving and giving without expecting will always lead to abundant blessings here on Earth and beyond. While it seems like anyone can display servanthood without training, that's not always the case. There must be a level of discernment to make wise decisions. Wisdom (see Appendix) is important because we must know how and when God wants to use us to help others. Today I went to a restaurant and a homeless man asked me to buy him something to eat. I had to ask the Holy Spirit for wisdom concerning the situation. We have to use the gift of discernment when we are in a position for decision making.

Jesus washing His Disciples' feet was the most amazing display of servanthood as we see in the following verses. John 13:1-5 (NIV) says, *"It was just before the Passover Festival. Jesus knew that the hour had come for him to leave this world and go to the Father. Having loved his own who were in the world, he loved them to the end. The evening meal was in progress, and the devil had already prompted Judas, the son of Simon Iscariot, to betray Jesus. Jesus knew that the Father had put all things under his power and that he had come from God and was returning to God; so he got up from the meal, took off his outer clothing, and wrapped a towel around his waist. After that, he poured water into a basin and began to wash his disciples' feet, drying them with the towel that was wrapped around him."*

This is a humble act of love to others.

There is an article that speaks to essential traits exhibited by a person and how that relates to character. The program discussed "Six Pillars of Character", is similar to core values of some large corporation. Most successful companies use: trustworthiness, respect, responsibility, fairness, caring, and citizenship to help attach business and develop model employees. James Hillman (1996)[4], in The Soul's Code: In Search of Character and Calling, describes the "invisible source of personal consistency, for which I am using the word 'habit,' psychology today calls character.

As I look back at all the times I have served other, the truth is my success as a servant leader today is a direct result of those experiences. Servant leadership really begins prior to becoming a leader.

If something lept in you when you read about the gift of leadership, take time to check your attitude! Yes, I said check your attitude to make sure there are no self-esteem issues and necessity to hold a leadership position or title. Who have you been able to influence and what was your purpose behind it? Was it for your gain? Stop right now and ask God to search your heart. You can start fresh and new, now that you know what your gifts are.

The Gift of Preaching

Another spiritual gift that is mentioned in the Bible is the gift of preaching. Do you feel that you have the gift of preaching? Then stop right where you are and say "Thank you Jesus!" The spiritual gift of pastor or pastor/shepherd is one that carries many different responsibilities. This gift is closely related to the spiritual gifts of leadership and teaching. Some say that because a person has the gift of preaching this does not necessarily make them a pastor. I say that once you have this gift you have the ability to lead people. The Greek word for pastor is *Poimen* and simply means shepherd or overseer.

Let's take a look at the specific method of Expository Preaching (I chose to discuss this style of preaching, because it appeals to me the most) and how it reminds me of something my Pastor said in our minister's meeting one Saturday. He expressed that we need to improve in our preaching by understanding that our audience has changed and increased. The church has recently been added to an organization you may know called "Faith Network" television broadcast and we can be seen in 94 million homes globally. Pastor stated that we are no longer preaching to a few people in our community, but now our audience is all over the world. In the book, Robinson[5] mentions that we must preach to the world addressed by the TV commentator, the newspaper columnist, the internet, and social media. Preaching requires intense study of the subject. The delivery must be educated, clear and concise. The word expository contains the word expose and this is what is done with this style of preaching. The text must be exposed in the original meaning of the text. Sometimes there are overlaps in this style and others.

Expository preaching will encourage you to study the Word of God in the purest form and therefore not having to modify what is being said. This will help, when preaching to Bible scholars or a group of students that are educated in the Word. This will be coupled with other forms of preaching to help ensure that students have a clear understanding of the message being delivered.

If this is your area of giftedness, then the planning process is the start to a good sermon. There are several steps that we will look at in this type of preaching.

The first step in Expository preaching is selecting your passage. It is important to know what you will be talking about. You can't build a sermon without a subject matter (Scripture). This takes prayer and careful consideration as Robinson states in his book "While all Scripture is profit, not all Scripture is profitable." (page 29)

Step two is directly related to selecting the passage, where the studying begins. Before the passage can be exposed to the learner or preached, the teacher/preacher must have a clear understanding that can only come from studying that selected passage and other passages related to the sermon topic.

Step three is to discover the exegetical idea. The word exegetical means of or relating to exegesis; explanatory; interpretative. This will lead to a clearer understanding of the passage overall.

Step four is related to the previous discovery first and then analyzing must follow. Once interpretation has occurred, the exegetical data must be analyzed. The preacher/teacher must ask themselves three questions and make sure they can be answered before moving onto the next step in the process. "What does this mean?" "Is it true?" and "What difference does it make?"

Formulating the homiletical idea is step five. In this step, the preacher considers the audience's knowledge and experience, think through their exegetical idea and state it in the most exact, memorable sentence possible. Robinson reminds us that we are not lecturing the people but talking to them.

Determining the sermon's purpose is the next step. As preachers, we have to be able to see the outcome of the sermon. What do we expect to happen as a result of the sermon? I believe that purpose should be something we look at when we have chosen the passage, Robinson believes that this step should follow the previous.

Once the sermon's purpose has been determined, now it's time to figure out how the purpose will be accomplished. There are three major components in this step. There is deductively, semi-inductively, or inductively.

Now it's time to outline the sermon, so how the purpose will be accomplished has been established.

Step nine is where the preacher/teacher will now fill in the sermon outline. This segment reminds me of when a book is being written. The outline is key in completing prominent information to the sermon. This step comes after the previous step, because it makes this portion easier and is consider filling in the meat of the sermon.

The preparation of the introduction and conclusion of the message is needed for the last step.

The gift of preaching and teaching can in some way go hand in hand. However is that the only gift that might be helpful from the pulpit? Gifts such as evangelist, exhortation, leadership, pastor, etc., can also be an asset to pulpit ministry. Keep in mind that not everyone has the gift of preaching, some people become motivated to try it at one time or another, but hopefully realize when it's not their area of giftedness. Do you see this gift operating in you?

The Gift of Teaching

How about the gift of teaching? Do you feel that you possess this spiritual gift? As I mentioned previously, this gift has been operating in me since I was ten years old, and I would gather the children in the basement of my parent's home and teach them. It's funny how our gifts operate in us, while we don't have a clue. There are times you will see that I use preaching and teaching interchangeably.

It is imperative that we take a look at the steps/process to Jesus' teaching. His approach is one that everyone with the gift of teaching should commit to adapting. If you have the gift of teaching, you would be more effective and successful in the use of this gift by following His example of being an excellent teacher.

There are times that I have sat in a classroom or through a sermon and wondered why can't I or other students stay awake. The class must be invigorating, exciting and full of good information. If you have the gift of teaching your students definitely have to feel a need for the information. As in a sermon, a student must recognize how what is being taught will change their life. They will soon understand that this information is needed and thereby transfer to a state of wanting it. Imagine if a classroom of students responded like those who learned from the Master teacher Himself. Students would feel a sense of pride, worth and confidence. They would be motivated and invigorated. What I love and appreciate about Jesus' teaching style is that He was willing and could teach anyone; even the Samaritan woman at the well. Not only was He not to drink from her, but not talk to her at all. There are preachers and teachers that won't preach or teach a certain group of people, but in Mark 16:15-16 (KJV) He said to them, *"Go into all the world and preach the gospel to all creation. Whoever believes and is baptized will be saved, but whoever does not believe will be condemned."* We are instructed in this manner of teaching and preaching. God did not say to go to certain areas only or preach only to one group of people. This scripture means to go everywhere and speak to everyone. This scripture brings us truth in the Word of God.

Jesus used a question to seize the attention of the students with saying "Give me a drink." Who does that? Only Jesus! He is an example of how we can approach a situation to get the best results. This manner captured the woman's attention and thereby stirred curiosity. I believe at this point the woman felt a need to hear more of what this Master Teacher had to say. It's like when our Pastor preaches, he comes out of the box with things that make the congregation say, "I want this", by using illustrations and theatrical examples. This is where the want turns into the need. The woman first felt the "want" to hear more from Jesus and then her desire created the "need" to hear what He had to say.

Recently I spoke on the gift of teaching and other spiritual gifts at a local conference. I utilized the method of music to stir and stimulate the "what's this", to seize the attention of the attendees. Since I was seeking to empower the women, the song was something that spoke to "girl power". I also followed Jesus' approach, by starting off with the question "What on earth am I here for?" This helps the learner to start thinking. With this gift we should be believing God for meeting the "real need" and have the students leave with the feeling of "I got what I wanted."

Dr. Bruce Wilkinson[6] speaks of seven Retention Maxims that must be explored with those that have the gift of teaching. Teachers must realize that it is their responsibility that the student retains the information learned. Some teachers have battled with these many times over. We have heard teachers say that it's not their fault if the student can't remember things taught to them, but this is a selfish way for a teacher to think. The teacher must find ways to evaluate if the student effectively understands what was taught or is being taught.

The teacher must be able to relate the content to real life situations. When connections to everyday situations are made, retention of the information becomes that more relevant to the learner. Maxim number five reminds us of how children begin to the learn at a young age. Think about when we first learn the alphabets. We said things like "A is for Apple", then we would be shown a photograph of an apple. The facts were arranged, we were provided with illustrations and the letters were arranged in a certain order.

We could think of actors that have to learn the lines of a script and may have done the same show and repeated the same lines for a certain period. These lines will be remembered for a long time to come. This can also be said for songs that we learn and sing repeatedly. If teaching is your gift you can use these techniques to become effective in operating in your gift.

If this is your area of giftedness, you must as teachers/preachers understand and intentionally act on effectively bringing clear and concise learning to the student. It is imperative for the teacher to research and get the necessary information; learn it to clearly communicate it. You can't teach something you don't know yourself. Wilkinson tell us that there must be overview of the subject, organization of the subject and an outline of the subject first (page 237).

The Retention Method must involve reducing the selected material and prioritize the information to be conveyed effectively. Considering the audience is key in selecting and minimizing the information to be taught.

While Wilkinson states that step three in the Retention Method should be to rearrange and simplify the package, we can also consider this to be a manipulation of the lesson to be taught. The need to rearrange the material for more effective delivery is important.

Step four in the Retention Method is what many teacher/preachers tend to struggle with. The memorization of material is sometimes difficult, especially when there are several lessons to prepare at the same time. The best thing is to become familiar with the material and practice it as much as you can in order to retain as much as you can.

Step five of the Retention Method allows the student to "master" the material taught. The content is applied in a manner that helps the student retain the information.

As I previously mentioned in Chapter 3, the method of illustration seems to be the most effective. There is power in communicating information through show and tell. Illustrations are extremely effective in teaching. I can relate to the illustration that my Pastors used to speak on tithing.

I enjoy using dramatizations in my teaching as a form of illustration to help my student retain information and aid in the development of the learning process. I have used drama to assist pastors in bringing the Word of God forth. This method is effective in assisting the student in retaining the information taught. While this is an effective approach, there are other approaches that may be effective based on a different audience or student group.

It is important for the teacher to know that he/she is responsible and key to the learner/student to retain the information being taught. Retention is directly connected to the motivation of the students. One of my methodologies of retention is to motivate the students by ensuring processes are in place for them to be able to easily access information. The learner/students would be able to get information at any time and not have to wait until they are in class. I currently allow my students to email me or text me at any time if

THE SPIRITUAL GIFTS OF THE SHEPHERD

there is a question they are not able to answer. Knowing this accessibility is available to my students, it motivates them to want to work harder and this helps with retention. It is important for teachers/preachers to have the goal of seeing their students succeed by any means necessary.

Since I do also operate in the gift of teaching, the second method I currently use with my students is the repetition and reciting method. Earlier this year I taught a class of twelve life coaches and I noticed it was difficult for some of the students to retain the information and almost checked out. I knew I could not have anyone drop out of class and decided to use the repetition method. I figured it was best to spend the rest of the time available to discuss the information already taught earlier that morning. The students were asked several questions repeatedly. This method was helpful in them being able to retain information and thereby they felt valuable and wanted to continue taking the class. The need to repeat information is evident in Wilkinson's book in Maxim six: Retention strengthens long-term memory through regular review; where he states that God created man with short-term memory and long-term memory (page 226).

The Law of Retention has helped me to increase my teaching skills and has given me a new way to be responsible for the students that I am given the opportunity to teach.

These two methods have been already proven through my utilization in previous classes.

If teachers use the steps that Jesus used in His teaching, they could master the craft and gain the excitement of the students. Teachers must learn their students. Teachers and preachers must know when to light the fire under the student and when to light the fire within. Both may have the same results, but the teacher will need to know which of these two fits the circumstance.

I was sharing with my husband the new revelation of the woman at the well and Jesus' approach in giving a command that seized her attention. She and others around knew that he should not have spoken to her, in a "normal" setting, but He did. I believe Jesus was already determining the theme response. This must be done by a teacher before teaching the lesson. "Give me a drink", He said, and it caught her off guard. This stirred her curiosity to want to know more, not just about this Man, but why He would speak to her and risk being ridiculed or be criticized. She wanted to know more about Him. He now had her attention.

The central idea of *Matthew 5:13 -16 says, "You are the salt of the earth. But if the salt loses its saltiness, how can it be made salty again? It is no longer good for anything, except to be thrown out and trampled underfoot. You are the light of the world. A town built on a hill cannot be hidden. Neither do people light a lamp and put it under a bowl. Instead, they put it on its stand, and it gives light to everyone in the house. In the same way, let your light shine before others, that they may see your good deeds and glorify your Father in heaven."*

This scripture shows us that as teachers we must be an example. When you think of salt, it is the most popular form of seasoning on the earth. It causes everything to taste better. It adds flavor to food and that's why this scripture is significant in showing us how we should be with teaching. We also should be a light on a hill, shining for the world to see.

When we as teachers live with this scripture in mind, we will stimulate the need, because the student will want more of what is being taught. It will also in some sense let the student know what they need at that moment. It will help distill the false need and bring forth the truth.

> *John 10:7-10 Then said Jesus unto them again, Verily, verily, I say unto you, I am the door of the sheep. All that ever came before me are thieves and robbers: but the sheep did not hear them.*
>
> *I am the door: by me if any man enter in, he shall be saved, and shall go in and out, and find pasture.*

The thief cometh not, but for to steal, and to kill, and to destroy: I am come that they might have life and that they might have it more abundantly.

In John 10:7-10 the main idea is to be like Jesus and lead the people into truth. Teachers and preachers are like shepherds that lead the sheep. Our teaching can lead people to the truth or away from the truth. We must teach those placed in our path with clarity, truth and by following Jesus' example.

Jesus was, is, and will always be the epitome of what an effective teacher should embody. He was focused on us, His students and the need to make sure we learned. He always created an atmosphere that was conducive to learning.

The three major relationships that directly impact the majority of all classroom situations are broken into first the "style", meaning how the teacher should teach. Teachers who find style to be important, enjoys what takes place in the process of teaching and learning. They would normally add excitement in the way they convey the information. They strive for spontaneity in teaching. Style is key in gaining and maintaining the attention of the student.

The relationship between what is taught is important for the teacher. This would be the content or subject matter. Teachers that are subject-oriented, tend to research in abundance and have more information than is usually needed.

Thirdly, the importance may be in who is being taught. When a teacher is student-focused, they tend to think of them as friends. They find the students interesting outside of class and may share life experiences with them and even go out to events together. The teacher may find these extraordinary activities as a way of helping the student to succeed. They usually know the names of their students.

The element of loving the student both consistently and unconditionally. The need to love the students in this manner is important. In the book, Wilkinson suggests that love includes passion. The need to express the subject by keeping the students' needs in mind. As an instructor, I tend to alter my style regularly, by studying my students. Teachers must have a level of confidence in their talents and gifts. The teacher must not try to be someone else but maintain their identity. It is key that teachers constantly pay attention to the attitudes and actions of their students. Teachers must use their strengths and allow them to overshadow their weaknesses, while also relying on the Holy Spirit to impart and teach. Relying on the Holy Spirit goes beyond teaching and taps into the supernatural.

Teachers must first consider what they anticipate or want the outcome to be, prior to preparing the lesson or sermon. We must work from the end to move towards the beginning. These are all important to keep in mind as a teacher prepares to effectively impact the students or learner.

The Pastoral Epistle

This Pastoral Epistles show pastoral concern for the recipients of the letters by Timothy and Titus. These pastoral matters involved the care of souls and the orderly conduct of God's people in the church as well as in the world.

The Pastoral Epistle regarding Timothy is quite intriguing as it relates to teaching and preaching. First, pointing out the fact that Paul entrusted young Timothy with such a task because he saw the gift of teaching upon Timothy. This caused some people to look down on the writing. The book mentions how Timothy being young, can help college-aged students and young people alike, to understand that young people zealous for Christ, willing to repent of their sins and trust in him, are ready to take up the cross and follow him is a costly service. This has today played a major role in the growth of God's kingdom. This is an encouragement to young people today. Those who have the gift of teaching can hone in on reaching this generation.

Paul begins with a fitting salutation, by greeting Timothy with his title, and who he was in Christ Jesus. He greeted him by saying "My dear son." This shows the caring nature towards Timothy. Paul furthermore, gives God thanks for who Timothy is in his life and talks about his grandmother

Lois and his mother Eunice. He shows that he is proud of Timothy for the person he is. Timothy is reminded by Paul to remain loyal to the Gospel and not be timid in the word. In 2 Timothy 1:6, Paul mentions Timothy should not be ashamed of him and join with him in suffering for the Gospel, through the power of God. This is the same manner for you with the gift of teaching. Do not be ashamed of sharing the Gospel.

In this same chapter, Paul urges Timothy to keep reminding the people of God to do their best and present themselves to God as one approved, hereby using his gift of teaching. They should avoid godless chatter because they will become more and more ungodly. Two teachers Paul mention are Hymenaeus and Phietus and how they have departed from the truth. These two were falsely teaching that the resurrection had already taken place, and they destroyed the faith of some of the people. It is necessary to ask God if the gift of teaching is upon you because you don't want to be like these two teachers Paul mention and falsely teach others.

There is also a level of maturity that comes with teaching. This does not happen overnight but will come with prayer and supplication. Timothy was young, therefore Paul urged him to flee the evil desires of youth and pursue righteousness, faith, love, and peace, along with those who call on the Lord out of a pure heart.

Paul ends his letter to Timothy, reminding him that in knowing his teaching, way of life, purpose, faith, patience, love, endurance, persecutions, sufferings, things that have happened to him in Antioch, Iconium, and Lystra, but God rescued him. He tells him that everyone who wants to live a godly life in Christ Jesus will be persecuted. He reminds Timothy to continue in what he has learned and be convinced of it.

Through today's teachings we as Christian, are to be reminded daily that ALL Scripture is God-breathed and is useful. We must use the Scriptures to teach, rebuke, correct, and train in righteousness to thoroughly equip the servants of God for every good work.

We have all experienced lessons or sermons that have left the student hanging. There was no conclusion and created a sense of lack of completion. It is key to conclude with the same purpose in which the lesson or sermon was started. In my opinion, the conclusion should be also a "call of action" to the student. This method is effective in assisting the student in retaining the information taught. While this is an effective approach, other approaches may be effective based on a different audience or student group as you grow in the gift of teaching. We must also seek to ensure the conclusion is true and relevant to the lesson or sermon from the beginning. It is imperative that we look at the lesson or sermon as an overall unit and not segment it in our conclusion. There also needs to be a purpose in our conclusion. Consider what is being said, why it is being said, and what effect are we expecting as you grow and improve in the gift of teaching.

It is important that we do not confuse the learner and possibly create the lesson or sermon to be ineffective. I have heard lessons or sermons where the preacher is concluding more than once. We must see our target of landing and know where we want to go. The conclusion takes time to plan and it must be a part of the overall goal-setting process. The best part of the conclusion is establishing a "call to action". If we don't encourage the learner to act, then our teaching/preaching could be deemed ineffective. Both may have the same results, but the teacher needs to know which of these two best fits the teaching forum. Those with the gift of teaching should be thorough in their lessons. The conclusion must contain a level of accountability for the student. It must inspire them to do something.

> *"The Son of Man did not come to be served, but to serve." (Matt. 20:28)*

Paul in 1 Corinthians

In 1 Corinthians 12:7, Paul reminds the Corinthians of gifts they possess; "Now to each one the manifestation of the Spirit is given for the common good." Another scripture tells us why we must use our spiritual gifts, Ephesians 4:12 "To prepare God's people for works of service, so that the body of Christ may be built up" and 1 Peter 4:10, instructs us that "Each one should use whatever gift he has received to serve others..."

   These scriptures remind us that we must be daring to act and respond. The most difficult part of using our gifts is first discovering that we have gifts. Sometimes I reflect on what life was like "pre-gift knowledge". For many years, I did not know what my purpose on earth was. I walked around, like many others, not knowing why God has me here. It's a dangerous thing to live without knowing your gifts. We can be purposeful only when we know who we are in Christ. When I think of "daring to act", I am reminded of a video of Steve Harvey saying that we must "jump" and not stay on the ledge of the mountain all our life.

   My gift of discernment and gift of prophecy (explained later) are two that I did not understand for a long time. I believe I was afraid to walk in these gifts. One day, I remember speaking into my Pastor's life. I shared some things that the Holy Spirit was depositing in me that day, just for the man of God. I was nervous about speaking to someone who speaks into the lives of many every day. Once I was done, Pastor told me to not be afraid to let God use me. He furthermore said to walk in my gifts boldly. That was a defining moment for me and I began to understand what God was doing in my life for His Glory.

Today, while out and about, I saw a woman and we immediately made eye contact. It was as though I could see straight through to her spirit. I began to speak the things the Holy Spirit was whispering to me. The woman was quite astonished and began to question, how I knew these things about her life. She sat in her seat shocked and puzzled yet she had the expression of love on her face. I would venture to say, she was amazed by how much God loves her, to send this lady (me) with answers she had been waiting on.

I continually have these experiences daily. I have learned to accept the gifts God has entrusted to me and share them with others. Again, it's trust and not ownership. I have met people, who once had a gift and then later on they can no longer operate in their gift. Some people say, "if you don't use it, you will lose it". I believe in some cases this may be true. We must exercise our gifts. For instance, if you have the gift of faith, you must exercise your faith. Not using our gifts can be a major loss, because it fuels our purpose. What will you tell God was the reason you never used your gifts to grow His Kingdom? It is important that we use the gifts that God has given to us to advance the Kingdom. The potential gain and/or losses of acting versus not acting for all parties involved is inevitable. We can gain a great reward or suffer a magnitude of losses by having our gifts lay dormant. I want to use every gift that He has entrusted to me and hear those words every Christian look forward to hearing one day "well done thy good and faithful servant."

Gift of Prophecy

Let's look at the gift of Prophecy which is to strengthen and encourages others. It creates stronger faith and uplifts the believer. The gift of prophecy can manifest Itself through preaching, teaching and other means. Prophecy should bring about edification.

> *"And now I commend you to God and to the word of His grace, which is able to build you up and to give you the inheritance among all those who are sanctified. Acts 20:32*

It is important to know that speaking in tongues does not give prophecy. Prophecy must be given in a language that others understand.

> *"Hear now My words: If there be a prophet among you, I the Lord will make Myself known unto him*

in a vision and will speak unto him in a dream."
Num. 12:6.

The gift of prophecy is a special gift that God gives through some Christians. This gift can be dangerous in the wrong hands. Those with the gift of prophecy is to apply the Word of God to a situation that change can occur. Prophets can be considered the messenger of the Body of Christ and do not compromise what they hear from the Holy Spirit or in dreams. Does God speak to you in dreams?

I believe that my mother had the gift of prophecy and the Holy Spirit spoke to her in dreams. Many people would ask her to interpret their dreams. When I was 4 years old, I was sitting on the front steps of my parent's store in Port of Spain, Trinidad, when a strange woman I had not remembered seeing before came and sat next to me. My parents were busy tending to customers and conducting business in the shop. The lady said words to me that I don't remember to this day. Later that evening I became ill and my parents had me transported to the local hospital. The halls seemed cold and the metal bed rail with the thin mattress did not seem welcoming. That night and the next few days the doctors worked diligently to discover what was going on with me. They said they had never seen such symptoms before. My parents began to worry, especially when the doctors said they could not do anything else for me and they felt my parents should prepare for the worst.

That night my mother cried herself to sleep, but while she slept God gave her a vision that provided the answers to my illness. When my parents returned to the hospital the next morning and shared what was told of my mother that night, the doctors had an ah-ha moment. It was clear to them and they were then able to treat me for my ailment. There were several other times when the Holy Spirit spoke to my mom in her dreams that bought clarity and edification.

Some think that the gift of prophecy can be defined as intuition, but it's much more than that. Some people tend to use and abuse this gift. Those that practice witchcraft, to believers and non-believers alike are mistaken for having the gift of prophecy. This gift is important to the Body of Christ.

I remember my aunt, whom I loved dearly being able to prophesy to others, but in a manner that bought fear upon them. She would say things that would cause them to do what she wanted. It was not until after her death I realized she was operating in witchcraft or what some call Obeah (the practice of witchcraft) in the Caribbean. You see, anything that tries to control another person comes from a spirit of witchcraft and is not of God.

I remember traveling to Trinidad for her funeral, and my maternal cousins driving my husband and I to her home in preparation to pack up her items. Since she had no children, this became the responsibility of my uncle and myself.

We pulled up to a neighborhood of huge three-story beautiful houses in an area of Port of Spain. My husband and I sat in the back seat of the car, while my cousins sat in the front. At the front of the house, we were greeted by tall flags that blew in the wind, high up to the second floor. I later learned that the flags represented some type of cult. My cousins quickly instructed us to remove all of our jewelry before exiting the vehicle. We complied because we lived in the United States and were not familiar with the surroundings. Standing at the corner were several young men, watching our every move as though we were easy prey. We ignored them and proceeded up the external steps headed to the third-floor apartment, where my aunt lived. The whole time the young men kept their eyes on us, not saying anything. We entered the apartment and a strange feeling came over me. It's as though the gift of prophecy was operating in me, but I had not connected the dots. It's as though discernment and prophecy were blending to form a tsunami of emotions within me. I proceeded to make my way to the bedroom as though something was pulling on me. My cousin said, "Don't go in there, you must be crazy." I realized there was a spirit of fear operating in her at that moment. I kept walking and she said, "I am not going in with you." The following scripture came to mind....

> *"For God hath not given us the spirit of fear; but*
> *of power, and of love, and of a sound mind." 2*
> *Timothy 1:7*

I was not afraid of my aunt, as I said. I loved her. After all, she was there for me through my teenage pregnancy; the only real support I had. I went into her bedroom and looked at her chester draws, photos and other things. I believe she had the gift of prophecy but used it in a manner that was something other than God speaking. You must never use your gift for manipulation and self-gain. God has entrusted us with these gifts to uplift the Kingdom. If we don't become clear of our purpose, then we will fail in living it out.

During my aunt's funeral, I realized that she was well respected and, in most cases, feared by those in her community. Those young men had stood and watched us as a way of protecting us from other bandits. People referred to my aunt as the Shango Baptist Priest. I sat back that day in the funeral parlor and saw things done that I still don't understand today and may never understand.

If the gift of prophecy is in you, you will know it. God will show you things that you sometimes won't understand, but when it begins to operate in you, you will get more clarity and operate in it.

As I write this section of the book, I am sitting on a plane occasionally glancing out the window as we ascend into the air above Myrtle Beach, South Carolina and going higher in altitude. I can't help but think of God's love for us that He gave us these gifts. He gave us such responsibilities to carry out this journey with purpose.

Some people in my life have a running joke of my gift of prophecy. You see sometimes when I am very tired the Holy Spirit will be speaking to me and I begin to prophecy to those He gives me a message for. Slowly I would fall asleep and then wake up and start to prophecy again. It's strange because I would speak in and out of sleep. Someone recently told me that a famous woman of God has this same type of manner in which the gift operates in her. Something to do with sleep and wake. I am still trying to figure it out. It's about connecting the dots, right? Do you think you have this gift?

Convictions and Superstitions that will hinder you from operating in your Spiritual Gifts

The Convictions that are little more than superstitions can keep you from discovering or not operating effectively in your spiritual gifts. Writing this book gave me the gumption to first explore the word conviction as related to the Bible.

The word conviction is used in the Bible as seen here in Acts 8:37 And Philip said, "If you believe with all your heart [if you have a conviction, full of joyful trust, that Jesus is the Messiah and accept Him as the Author of your salvation in the kingdom of God, giving Him your obedience, then] you may. And he replied I do believe that Jesus Christ is the Son of God."

The Merriam-Webster dictionary gives us the definition of conviction as such; the act of convincing a person of error or of compelling the admission of a truth; the state of being convinced of error or compelled to admit the truth. It is necessary to know the definition of the word to get a clear understanding of the terminology used in this paper.

The same said dictionary defines superstitions as; a belief or practice resulting from ignorance, fear of the unknown, trust in magic or chance, or a false conception of causation; an irrational abject attitude of mind toward the supernatural, nature, or God resulting from superstition.

Some believe that conviction comes when the conscience is convicted, and a certain feeling takes place that creates emotions. Being convicted can also be a realization that as a Christian you have sinned. Conviction is being convinced of wrongdoing against God, sinning. These are two major reasons Christian fail to operate in their gifts.

It amazes me how some Christians have certain

superstitions. These are beliefs which we sometimes practice. Growing up in a Caribbean home, there were many superstitions. Sometimes I find myself doing or saying certain things my mother did. For instance, when a baby would get the hiccups, we were told to take a piece of thread, fold it up, wet it and place it on the head of the baby. The strange thing is that the hiccupping would subside. Even superstitions like if you walk under a ladder, or breaking a mirror, or other beliefs. These things took place in a Christian home and yet we still practiced them. The African heritage also brings with it many superstitions that are still practiced by Christians today. Whenever I find myself participating in a superstitious act, I become convicted. This makes me know that superstition is not of God. He gives us discernment, wisdom, knowledge and understanding and these things transcend our belief in His word.

Some convictions attract attention to a selfish ego. When I think of selfish ego, I think of the week we studied simplicity in one of my online classes. I believe that simplicity is the opposite of ego. The importance of simplicity and humility contrasts with walking with an ego. When we make up our mind to "deny ourselves, take up our cross and follow Christ", we cannot do so with an ego. Jesus tells the disciple in Matthew 16:24-26, then Jesus told his disciples, "If anyone would come after me, let him deny himself and take up his cross and follow me. For whoever would save his life will lose it, but whoever loses his life for my sake will find it. For what will it profit a man if he gains the whole world and forfeits his soul? Or what shall a man give in return for his soul?"

We cannot walk in servanthood and live an egotistical life. As I mentioned previously, servanthood is a lifestyle and Jesus' life is the perfect example of how to walk in it.

The leaders at our Church have learned to walk in humility and we are reminded that ego is not an option. Our Pastor demonstrated this by washing our feet during ordination. It was humbling for our Pastor to display such a selfless act in the presence of a room full of attendees. He continues to shepherd us in the same manner. We are all human and may occasionally feel our "peacock" feathers start to rise in certain situations, but because we are following Jesus, we are immediately convicted.

These convictions are key, and one example is in the Bible is in 1 Peter 5:5, *"All of you, clothe yourselves with humility toward one another, because, God opposes the proud but gives grace to the humble"*. We must walk in humility, conviction and simplicity if we say we are following Christ. I thank God for forgiving time and time again. He has also given us the gift of conviction to know when we have sinned against Him, which gives us the opportunity of repentance.

CHAPTER 5

WHICH OF THESE GIFTS MAKES YOUR HEART LEAP?

This can be possibly be answered by taking a look at areas you have served in. This can be in church or the secular world. For instance, if you are a teacher in the public-school system and love your job. You enjoy imparting information to the children. This is a clear sign that you have the gift of teaching. There could also be the gift of knowledge sitting dormant and needs to be activated. Salvation is important for these gifts to be active and operational in the Body of Christ.

Love must be a selfless act.

Last July was emotionally difficult as we laid to rest one of the missionaries I had served with in Haiti less than two months prior. This situation made me reflect on the opportunities I feel I have lost in learning from our dear mother of missions. We had known each other for a short time and I could not understand her toughness towards us as new missionaries. She was a praying woman and loved the Lord with all her heart. She held many nuggets of wisdom and we learned things from her that we will treasure forever.

I can't help but reflect and think of the things I could have done to create a better relationship with her and learned from the many gifts God entrusted to her. If there is anything I wish about our relationship, is that I had taken the time to get to know her more. I remember placing the people in her room on our trip that needed mentorship. I felt she would impart wisdom and knowledge into them and they needed that, but know that I look back, I needed that. I could have done more to get to know her and absorb her knowledge of missions and life as a mother, grandmother and wife.

Her passing made me think of how we get busy doing ministry work and not take time to minister to one another, through love and communication while using our spiritual gifts. It's ironic how we forget about the people right at our disposal. Everything we need is around us. There are people with similar gifts that can help strengthen your gifts.

To fully function in our gifts, we must have biblical love, the most passionate love can be found in Romans 5:8, where God's has shown for us as sinners; *"...commendeth his love toward us, in that, while we were yet sinners, Christ died for us."* This is a clear indication that God loves us even in our imperfections. Even when we rebel and don't live the life He expects of us, He still loves us. God is not emotional about loving us. If He were, we would be in a terrible situation. God loves us in a way that no one else could ever love us. He gave His only begotten son to die on the cross that we may have life and have it more abundantly.

God has healed my heart about not getting to know Mother Dorothy when I had the opportunity. He has given me other chances to love and build relationships with those He placed in my path. I will work to not make the same mistake and not miss the mark of loving those around me. I pray the same for you.

Love is the connection to operating in our gifts!

The word "love" can be defined by many people in various terms. It's like some people think of love as what they feel and not what they do for others. Some people feel that love must be reciprocal; for them to give it, they must get it first. Love must be a selfless act.

God's love is not based on what we do or what we say, but He loves us unconditionally. True love is not possible without God, because 1 John 4:8 tells us that "...God is love." Love is not money, clothing, cars, houses or other material things.

The Apostle Paul in, 1 Corinthians 13:4-8, describes the love of Jesus Christ. In this scripture he says, "Love is patient, love is kind. It does not envy, it does not boast, it is not proud. It does not dishonor others, it is not self-seeking, it is not easily angered, it keeps no record of wrongs. Love does not delight in evil but rejoices with the truth. It always protects, always trusts, always hopes, always perseveres. Love never fails. But where there are prophecies, they will cease; where there are tongues, they will be stilled; where there is knowledge, it will pass away. God lets us know in this scripture that biblical love (the only true love), cannot fail. When love is about emotions, it will fail every time and not last."

1 Corinthians 13:4-8 is a guide on how we should love one another. If we used this scripture in our relationships with others, it will help foster positive relationships with others. Let's use marriage as an example in this case. We must be patient with our spouses. Sometimes they may not be everything or do things we expect them to, but that does not negate the fact that we are to love them. We are to be

one in a marriage and therefore if we envy our spouse, we are only envying ourselves. The most profound part of this scripture to me is "keep no record of wrongs." Some couples have a way of bringing up past wrongs in arguments, yet they say they have forgiven their spouse. God does not bring up our past wrongdoings. The many times we have sinned, the many times we have done wrong and the many times we sinned against His word. The way He loves and forgives us, we are to love our brother and sister. Jesus gives us a directive in John 13:34-35, "A new command I give you: Love one another. As I have loved you, so you must love one another. By this everyone will know that you are my disciples if you love one another."

I recently preached a sermon and spoke to the people of the importance of praying for others. This is an act of love. We are to pray for our friends, family and enemies as well. We have to earnestly pray and ask God to touch their hearts and have them live the way He wants them to live. We should not ask God to hate them or to make them do what you desire them to do for you. God is a God of love and order. The most selfless way to display love for someone else, especially those that have done you wrong, is to pray for them.

There are a few words in the Bible that defines what love is. When I think of biblical love, the word agape comes to mind. It's a word I came to understand many years ago when I worked for a daycare center owned and operated by a pastor and his wife. The name of the daycare center was Agape Christian Day Care Center. This center was a place that was created to show love to children while in the care of the staff at this center. I learned about love for children and how to provide that love. Let's explore some of the words in the Bible that relate to love.

Agapoa is a word used to describe God's divine love for us and the word Agape is derived from it. We see this in John 3:16, "For God so loved the world, that he gave his only begotten Son, that whosoever believeth in him should not perish, but have everlasting life." This scripture shows God's total commitment to man. He gave His son, to die on the cross because He loves us that much.

The second word is Phileo and when translated it means love. It describes love for another person. This can be seen in John 21:15-17 as Jesus asked Peter, "Do you agape me more than the other disciples. Peter replied, "Yea, Lord; thou knowest that I love (phileo) thee". Knowing the meaning of both Agape and Phileo, Peter does not use the word Agapoa in this case.

The next word is Eros, which refers to sexual love. People may use the term "making love." This meaning is different from the first two words.

While there is different terminology that expresses love, God's biblical love is the only real love and the kind that we should strive to achieve as Christians. It should be something that comes easy. I often ask God to make me a river of love, that it may flow to others. I want when I enter a room people can feel the love that radiates from my presents. I thank God for loving me and giving His Son Jesus for the World.

I continue to learn about my gifts and how God allows me to operate in them. For almost eleven years, I have worked in the church as a Ministry Consultant. I have scheduled, requested Spiritual Gift Interviews with new members to find their gifts and begin to serve the people of God. My gifts of encouragement help me to ensure a level of comfort and peace with those in our meetings. The word encouragement is also associated with the Greek word paracletes. I am also a paracletes counselor, thereby interchanged would read "encouragement counselor". The gift of encouragement operates effectively in my life coaching practice.

My gift of Administration coupled with my gifts of discernment and encouragement all work together to help me in my ministry as well as personal life. There is a lot that is required in having the gift of administration.

If you find it easy to plan and execute events almost effortlessly, the gift of administration may be operating in you. Did something just leap inside of you? If it did, start operating in your gifts today! It is important that we pray and ask God for wisdom, knowledge and understanding in using our gifts and ensure we don't abuse them. Your gifts help you to excel in many areas of your life, including professional and personal. You will continuously learn how to effectively use your spiritual gifts and core values to live on purpose. The spiritual gifts God has blessed you with, are directly collated with the core values of commitment, loyalty, optimism, nurturing and trust. Having the opportunity to take a closer look at your spiritual gifts and values as a result of reading this book, I hope that it has given you clarity on why you are here on Earth and bringing God all the Glory.

CHAPTER 6

NOW THAT YOU KNOW YOUR GIFTS, WHAT'S NEXT?

R emember this:

SPIRITUAL GIFTS + PASSION = PURPOSE

Our gifts were not entrusted to our care for us to hold on to them. We must be unselfish in our giftedness. Whether in Church or out of Church, these gifts are for others. They are not to be used to mistreat others or take advantage of others. When we stand before God one day, we don't want to have to say, "God here are your gifts back, I was not able to use them". God would not be pleased with the lack of care of His gifts. This reminds me of the master in the bible, who gave his servants talents and was displeased with the way one of them used what he was given.

Matthew 5:16

In the same way, let your light shine before others, so that they may see your good works and give glory to your Father who is in heaven.

This scripture is a good definition of excellence and what God expects of us from a biblical standpoint. Excellence is manifested in God's Word.

Growing people and measuring ministerial excellence is a slow process as you operate in your gifts but is not at all impossible. In the fore-mentioned Scripture (Acts 2:42), the earlier church was not merely devoting itself to common activities but to a vital, spiritual relationship with people to ensure excellence. It was this relationship that produced active sharing in other ways. Many Christians; have gotten this backwards—that the activities produce the relationship with others. This is not true! The relationship comes first, the common activities to ensure excellence follows as we operate in our spiritual gifts.

It is vital for you to strive to go beyond mediocrity. The importance of building a total Quality Spiritual Culture within the church and your life lies in recognizing that you have incredible potential and we must discover our level of potential to strive for excellence. Be encouraged as you operate in your spiritual gifts and seek to encourage someone else. If God lives in you, it is your duty to love others, because He first loved you! The way to strive for excellence is by following the ways of Jesus and how He and still is the Master of excellence. You must seek to continue working in excellence that will help us be effective in the gifts God has entrusted to you. Don't leave all the responsibility on the pastor. Say this with me "DO SOMETHING"!

It is imperative that all in the Body of Christ, play a part in developing the Spiritual Arena of a Church striving for excellence.

Once you know your gift, now it's time to couple it with your passion.

The Application

> *Proverbs 24:16 The righteous may fall seven times but still get up, but the wicked will stumble into trouble.*

> *If you fail, keep trying and you will birth purpose.*

Now that I have gotten that out the way, let's talk *trying until you get it right*! Ok, so I always have a story, right? Yes, because our stories are to share with others. The fact that we have overcome those obstacles is evident that God was operating all along. We are to use our experience to help others know that God can and will do it for them, just as he did for you!

Passion is relative to the heart. Passion can be summed up to that one thing you would do, even if you did not get paid for it. Money is the last thing on your mind when you have a passion for something. Let me be open here: I was introduced to my passion for acting at the age of 14. I was a youth member of the National Council of Negro Women, in Queens New York. The program was called "Youth in Motion". We would get together each week with youth throughout the community and leaders that had a passion to help us discover who we are. At that time my mentor made a lasting impact on me. She saw in me back then, what I could not see in myself at the time. She helped schedule time at the local Community facility "Langston Hughes Library in Corona, where I was allowed to utilize the stage on the second floor. There I was able to direct plays, develop concerts and showcase my talent of Acting and Directing. I would gather all of my friends in the community and tell them that I am a director/producer and want them to be a part of my project. I would put shows on for free and help develop the skills of those in the production. Langston Hughes Library provided an atmosphere that was conducive to developing my gifts and passion. Here is the crazy thing about it, I did not know anything about gifts or passion and that I even had any. That's how a lot of adults are today. Some people go through life never connecting the dots. Don't be discouraged, because the fact that you are reading this book, tells me there is still time for you to live out what God has called you to do in this life. At that young age of 14, the NCNW would take us to see some major Broadway productions, such as ANNIE, CATS, DREAMGIRLS and more. We sat in nose-bleed seats, but I was grateful to be in the house (somebody say amen!). I would cheer as I sat at the edge of my seat and have my "wow" moments, wondering, how did all this come together.

I remember watching Jennifer Holiday sing her heart out and Sheryl Lee Ralph's act and the set turning the way it did, thinking "how in the world" did that happen? You see, the passion was operating in me, but I still did not connect the dots. My parents did not have a clue about what was brewing inside of me. That's why it is important to watch our children at a young age because there is passion brewing inside of them. My parents, being strict, old school, Caribbean mother and father, would have thought I lost my natural mind if I came to them saying "I want to be an actress". I remember going to them, saying that I want to try out for the High School of Performing Arts, where the majority of the cast of FAME attended at that time in Manhattan. It was my last year of Junior High School (8th grade) and this thing was stirring inside of me called Passion. Well, the worse thing is not to be prepared. My parents allowed me to audition for the High School of Performing Arts. That Saturday morning in 1979, we got in the car and set out for the audition. As we drove over the 59th Street Bridge and I looked out the window onto Roosevelt Island, I was excited about my future as an actress. I would be in Hollywood in no time and provide for my parents. We arrived at the school very early in the morning and the line seemed to wrap around the building. I could not believe how many young aspiring actors, dancers, singers and artists there were in the world. I was not the only one; a rude awakening moment for me. We checked in and took a seat. My monologue for the audition was from "THE GLASS MENAGERIE" and I was ready. I heard my name called and my palms became sweaty, my knees seemed to buckle, and I got up from the seat. My voice could barely be heard when I responded "here". My mom kissed me and said, "Ok, go ahead". I followed the woman into the room and was now facing a panel of three people. No one said anything about an audition with this many people. Well, there I was, as they started to the process, by asking me questions, which I later found out what slating meant. Let's just say that I realized while I had a gift/talent, I did not do anything to develop it. I bombed that audition, because of not being prepared and understanding what was inside of me. I stood in front of professionals in the arts and was not prepared. We must know who we are, whose we are and what we have inside of us. I will never forget the rejection that I felt as we drove back home that day. Thinking *what a fool I was*! Thinking, how could I believe I was called for this? I later realized that my passion could not be developed without my gifts. I had to understand my gifts first. It was like putting the horse before the cart.

Our gifts and passions must be developed for master operation. You see failure is alright as long as we get ourselves back up and keep it moving. The songwriter says, "We fall down, but we get up again." Failure is bound to happen because it strengthens us for our purpose. As I mentioned previously, many leaders in the Bible failed at one time or another, but they learned from it and kept going. The key is to be willing to go forward. Imagine yourself walking down a road, with all the people of the world toward something. There are bumps in that road that you may stumble on and hit your pinky toe. That really hurt! It's alright to sit on the curb for a minute and rub the toe, but make sure not to stay there. Get up and keep moving, because life does not stop happening. Life is like a wide road, with people walking towards something,

Keep pushing towards your goals. Keep your faith in God and not in man. He will pick you up, clean you off, and get you back on the right path.

You may be in a place where you need to mature and develop your gifts and passion. You should start by finding ways to learn more about your gifts. Find a good God-fearing mentor and watch them serve at your church. Maybe join the Sunday school class and look for a ministry where you can serve and learn. Maybe the typical men or women's Ministry?

What if I have been hurt and need healing first?

I know that 'church hurt 'can be the most difficult hurt to overcome. The old saying that "hurt people, hurt other people" is true. I suggest you pray and ask God to heal your heart. Don't let this stop you from having a relationship with God. He has healed others and He can heal you too.

What if I know my gifts?

Once you know your gift, now it's time to couple it with your passion. Make sure you know your passion and start serving. One good way of finding your passion is thinking on that one thing that you would do, even if you did not get paid for it. Like me, I would direct stage plays, even if I did not get paid to do it. Passion is that one thing that will wake you up at two a.m. in the morning to perfect it. Passion is that one thing that makes your heart leap! Make sure you have a passion for it! We are responsible for others. Yes, as hard as that may sound, we are responsible for others.

Don't be selfish with your gifts or your passion. One of my mentors, Dr. Patricia Bailey recently said at the SEW (Sisters Empowering the World) conference that "SELFISHNESS HAS AN ODOR, BUT SELFLESSNESS HAS A FRAGRANCE"! How do you smell?

Two years ago, on our twenty-ninth wedding anniversary, my husband asked me what I wanted to do to celebrate. I told him that I would like to visit a friend of mine who at the time was in federal prison in West Virginia. My husband is amazing, because he said, "Let's do it!" This friend of mine is very important and has been instrumental in helping me connect the dots to my purpose. We have been friends for over sixteen years and I am Godmother to two of her beautiful children. That Sunday afternoon, as we drove through the mountains of West Virginia to Aderson Prison Camp, I thought of what we would talk about when I got there. The emotions that I felt that day were overwhelming at times. We arrived at Aderson two hours later and I'm grateful to God for the three hours I was able to spend with her on such a special day. She's an amazing woman. During that time, she used her gifts, passion and purpose to minister to me. I thought it to be such a selfless act, that during her tough situation, she was at peace. As my husband and I had a silent ride back to Roanoke, Virginia, I cried tears of joy for my friend. This was one of the greatest examples of a selfless act I had experienced. It was proof that gifts, passion and purpose can still operate in what seems like a dry place. She had a selfless fragrance that seemed to fill the room. She knew her gifts.

What if I am already operating in my gifts?

While this is a place to be, it is necessary to examine ourselves every two years (at least) and take a Spiritual Gift Assessment (can be found in book stores or on-line). This will determine if our gifts may have shifted. Our gifts may shift in order of priority, based on things that we experience in life. We want to always make sure that we are being effective in the now!

What if there is not a ministry that can use my gifts?

I shared with you, how I started businesses, women's groups and a school. YOU CAN DO THE SAME THING! You can go to your Pastor and share your interest in starting a new ministry. For instance, if you have the gift of Administration and a Passion for the homeless, but your church does not have a food pantry. You can develop a plan to start a food pantry. It takes administration to start up anything you do in ministry. This same concept can be used outside of the church. Maybe there is a need in your community for a pantry? You can start a non-profit organization that could change the lives of homeless people in your community. Do something today!

CHAPTER 7

WALKING AND OPERATING IN YOUR GIFTS

When you start operating in your spiritual gifts and truly following what God has called you to do, then Biblical success is inevitable. Take a look at these five scriptures that should remind you of what God has for you! Biblical success comes once you have *"connected the dots to your purpose."*

5 scriptures or passages that speak to a Biblical understanding of success

> *Philippians 4:13 I can do all this through him who gives me strength.*

> *Psalms 37:4 Take delight in the LORD, and he will give you the desires of your heart.*

Proverbs 16:3 Commit to the LORD whatever you do, and he will establish your plans.

1King 2:3 and observe what the LORD your God requires: Walk in obedience to him, and keep his decrees and commands, his laws and regulations, as written in the Law of Moses. Do this so that you may prosper in all you do and wherever you go.

Deuteronomy 8:18 But remember the LORD your God, for it is he who gives you the ability to produce wealth, and so confirms his covenant, which he swore to your ancestors, as it is today.

These scriptures are a good definition of success from a biblical standpoint. Real success is manifested in God's Word. In the world, we are taught that success comes from working hard and having prominent careers. Some people work hard for most of their life span and still don't achieve success. We live in a society that uses statements to motivate others such as "the early bird catches the worm", "hard work pays off", "for every cloud there is a silver lining", and other sayings. We find that people try to live up to these statements in an effort of being successful.

We also tell children, with hard work, they can be

president or hold other high positions. We are doing them an injustice and possibly promoting false hope. These are statements used by Christians as well as non-Christians. We fail to realize that our true value lies in our wisdom, strength and performance which all comes from God. The ultimate passage of success in the Bible comes from Jesus' Parable of the Talent in Matthew 25:14-30. Here Jesus teaches that the kingdom of heaven is like a man going on a long journey. The man leaves and gives his three servants different amounts of money, measured by talents. To the first servant, the man gives five talents, to the second two talents, and to the last one talent—each according to his ability.

Upon his return, the Master asks what they did with the money. The first and second servants doubled their investments and received their master's praise. The third servant, who was given one talent, safeguarded the money but did nothing to increase it. As a result, he was condemned by the master for his inactivity.

The Parable of the Talents teaches us that true success comes in wisdom from God. We are to work, using our talents to glorify God, to serve his children and to further His kingdom. Money does not equate to success, but wisdom, knowledge and understanding, are the foundation of true success. Can God trust you with the gifts He gave to you for His people?

The Parable

Matthew 25:14-30 "Again, it will be like a man going on a journey, who called his servants and entrusted his wealth to them. 15 To one he gave five bags of gold, to another two bags, and to another one bag, each according to his ability. Then he went on his journey. 16 The man who had received five bags of gold went at once and put his money to work and gained five bags more. 17 So also, the one with two bags of gold gained two more. 18 But the man who had received one bag went off, dug a hole in the ground and hid his master's money. 19 "After a long time the master of those servants returned and settled accounts with them. 20 The man who had received five bags of gold brought the other five. 'Master,' he said, 'you entrusted me with five bags of gold. See, I have gained five more.' 21 "His master replied, 'Well done, good and faithful servant! You have been faithful with a few things; I will put you in charge of many things. Come and share your master's happiness!' 22 "The man with two bags of gold also came. 'Master,' he said, 'you entrusted me with two bags of gold; see, I have gained two more.' 23 "His master replied, 'Well done, good and faithful servant! You have been faithful with a few things; I will put you in charge of many things. Come and share your master's happiness!' 24 "Then the man who had received one bag of gold came. 'Master,' he said, 'I knew that you are a hard man, harvesting where you have not sown and gathering where you have not scattered seed. 25 So I was afraid and went out and hid your gold in the ground. See, here is what belongs to you.' 26 "His master replied, 'You wicked, lazy servant! So you knew that I harvest where I have not sown and gather where I have not scattered seed? 27 Well then, you should have put my money on deposit with the bankers, so that when I returned I would have received it back with interest. 28 " 'So take the bag of gold from him and give it to the one who has ten bags. 29 For whoever has will be given more, and they will have an abundance. Whoever does not have, even what they have will be taken from them. 30 And throw that worthless servant outside, into the darkness, where there will be weeping and gnashing of teeth.'

Money does not equate to success; wisdom, knowledge and understanding are the foundation of true success.

Excellence and Success in your gifts

Sometimes there seems to be a thin line between success and excellence. We as Christians must realize that both are not equal. I believe that success is an accomplishment and completing tasks or the ultimate task. Whereas, excellence is the substance used to achieve success. God wants us to succeed but do so in excellence as we operate in the gifts He has given to us.

One of my former pastors would say to us often "Do things in decency and in order". Therefore, we sought to always live up to those expectations as a mandate from God Himself. Success as Christians is not the ability to measure our accomplishments with the accomplishments of those around us. The false look at success is being like the "Jones's" and striving to have what others have. Again, embrace your own gifts and celebrate the gifts of others.

We tend to use the achievement of others to measure our

own success. What you see on social media is not always true!

Look at how athletes strive to break records of others. We see this in the book of Guinness World Records. Someone is always trying to measure success by beating someone else in a particular area. Humans are naturally competitive by nature. In Christ, we do not need to compete with one another. God has given us all gifts as I said before.

I believe that excellence fuels the vehicle that achieves success. While success seems competitive with others, excellence seems to be competition with ourselves. Through excellence, we strive to be the best we can be. Excellence is valuable and simply means to put our best foot forward. Each day it is important to strive for excellence. We may have failed yesterday, but today is a new day and excellence can be implemented again. Do you want to be excellent? God has already given you the tools to achieve excellence! Use your gifts!

Success is to attain a desired object or desired result and it does not mean that you are doing your best. You must apply Godly principles to achieve success in your own life. Scriptures are models for how God wants you to live and be successful in His eyes. Living the way God expects us to and following in Jesus' Footsteps is the way to a successful life while operating in your gifts.

When in doubt I find it necessary to revisit the scriptures mentioned on success, such as:

Philippians 4:13 I can do all this through him who gives me strength.

Psalms 37:4 Take delight in the LORD, and he will give you the desires of your heart.

Proverbs 16:3 Commit to the LORD whatever you do, and he will establish your plans.

1King 2:3 and observe what the LORD your God requires: Walk in obedience to him, and keep his decrees and commands, his laws and regulations, as written in the Law of Moses. Do this so that you may prosper in all you do and wherever you go

Deuteronomy 8:18 But remember the LORD your God, for it is he who gives you the ability to produce wealth, and so confirms his covenant, which he swore to your ancestors, as it is today.

Unlike success, to excel means to continue to improve or develop in your area of spiritual giftedness. Strive for excellence in your life each day. I often apply the phrase my previous pastor used often "do everything in decency and in order" and I admonish you to do the same. I realize that excellence is a prerequisite for success. You may miss the mark sometimes, but there is time to start over each day.

Sometimes using the phrase "What would Jesus do" can assist a person to strive for excellence. Excelling to live a life like Jesus did, such as loving everyone and treating people right is a continuous process. The word excel is derived from the Latin word *excellere*, which means to rise. This makes me think of my favorite poem by **Maya Angelou "Still I Rise"**.

The importance to excel like some in the Bible

I believe that Noah excelled by managing to build an ark that was capable of carrying many wildlife during a major flood. This flood resulted in catastrophic conditions for mankind. He did what God told him to do with excellence and therefore was able to carry out the mission. Noah had a great reward in (Genesis 6:8-9) But Noah found favor in the eyes of the LORD. These are the records of the generations of Noah. Noah was a righteous man, blameless in his time; Noah walked with God. Noah was operating in his gifts.

Joseph was 7 the first time he had his dreams about ruling over his family. I see Joseph as being one of the most successful men in the Bible. Joseph went through many adversities, but God delivered him out of each one. This is a perfect example of the difference in excelling and succeeding. Due to his many hardships, Joseph was not in a position to excel, but God gave him supernatural favor over his brothers. He gave him dreams and visions that caused much success in his situations. "Joseph is a fruitful vine, a fruitful vine near a spring, whose branches climb over a wall" (Genesis 49:22 NIV). That is the testimony of the Bible. "The LORD was with Joseph… The LORD blessed the Egyptian's house on account of Joseph… The LORD was with Joseph… The LORD was with him, and whatever he did, that the LORD made to prosper" (Genesis 39: 2, 5, 21). Joseph was operating in his gifts.

Now it's time for you to operate in your gifts. Remember I said at the beginning of this book that you will find your spiritual gift after reading it? Well, my prayer is that you have connected the dots to your purpose. God loves you in a mighty way that He spoke to me about including this spiritual gift test in the next few pages to help you confirm what has caused you to leap inside. I encourage you to take the spiritual gift assessment and see what your three top spiritual gifts are. Remember that gifts and talents are two different things. Talents are those things we do well, like dance, sing etc. These talents are usually our passions. Again, **SPIRITUAL GIFTS + PASSION = PURPOSE.**

124

Here is an example that should help you to discover and operate in your gifts. If you have the gift of encouragement and the talent to sing, then you will use your talent of singing to bring encouragement to others. You are living on purpose and have connected the dots. May God continue to richly bless you on your journey to spiritual growth.

APPENDIX

GIFT DEFINITIONS AND THEIR DISTINCTIVE QUALITIES

A = Administration (Efficiency)

Anointing for organizing, planning, bringing order out of chaos; coordinating and developing strategies to reach identified goals; bringing efficiency and effectiveness.

> *Exodus 18:1-24 And when Moses' father-in-law saw all that he did to the people, he said, What is this thing that thou doest to the people? Why sittest thou thyself alone, and all the people stand by thee from morning unto even? The thing that thou doest is not good. I will give thee counsel, and God shall be with thee: be thou for the people to Godward, that thou mayest bring counsel, and God shall teach them ordinances and laws,... Moreover thou shalt provide out of all the people able men, such as fear God, men of truth, hating covetousness; and place such over them,...and let them judge the people at all seasons; and it shall be, that every great matter they shall bring unto*

thee, but every small matter they shall judge…So Moses hearkened to the voice of his father-in-law and did all that he had said.

AA = Apostleship (New Ministries)

Anointing for pioneering new ministries/churches, ministering to the unreached in other cultures or communities, having authority and vision; entrepreneurial and adventurous.

Acts 13:2-3 As they ministered to the Lord, and fasted, the Holy Ghost said, Separate me Barnabas and Saul for the work whereunto I have called them. And when thy had fasted and prayed and laid their hands on them, they sent them away.

C = Craftsmanship (Skill)

Anointing for creatively designing/constructing items for use in ministry; skillful use of tools and materials (wood, cloth, paint, metal, etc.); practical, resourceful, and creative.

Exodus 31:1-6 And the LORD spoke unto Moses saying,…and I have filled him with the spirit of God, in wisdom, and in understanding, and in knowledge, and in all manner of workmanship, to devise cunning works, to work in gold, and in silver, and in brass, and in cutting of stones, to set them, and in carving of timber, to work in all manner of workmanship.

CC = Creative Communication (Artistic Expression)

Anointing for using art forms to communicate the gospel: drama, writing, art, music, etc; expressive, imaginative, artistic, unconventional, uses variety and creativity.

2 Samuel 6:1-15 And David danced before the LORD with all his might and David was girded with a linen ephod. So David and all the house of Israel brought up the ark of the LORD with shouting, and with the sound of the trumpet.

D = Discernment (Clarity)

Anointing for distinguishing truth from error; identifying deception and motives in others accurately, perceptive, insightful, intuitive, challenging, decisive, and truthful.

> *Acts 5:1-4 But a certain man named Ananias, with Sapphira his wife, sold a possession, And kept back part of the price, his wife also being privy to it, and brought a certain part, and laid it at the apostles' feet. But Peter said, Ananias, why hath Satan filled thine heart to lie to the Holy Ghost and to keep back part of the price of the land? Thou hast not lied unto men, but unto God.*

E = Encouragement (Exhortation)

Anointing for presenting the truth to comfort, strengthen, reassure, urge others to action, motivate, affirm, support, and encourage confidence in God's will.

> *Acts 11:22-24 Then tidings of these things come unto the ears of the church which was in Jerusalem and they sent forth Barnabas, that he should go as far as Antioch Who, when he came, and had seen the grace of God, was glad, and exhorted them all, that with purpose of heart they would cleave unto the Lord For he was a good man, and full of the Holy Ghost and of faith and much people was added unto the Lord.*

EE = Evangelism (The Good News)

Anointing for sharing the gospel with unbelievers so they respond; seeking out the lost, challenging unbelievers to faith in Christ, candid, sincere, persuasive, and confident.

> *Act 8:26-38 And the angel of the Lord spake unto Philip, saying, Arise and go toward the south unto the way that goeth down from Jerusalem unto Gaza, which is desert. And he arose and went: and, behold, a man of Ethiopia,...sitting in his chariot read Isaiah the prophet, Then the Spirit said unto Philip, Go near, and join thyself to this*

chariot, And Philip ran thither to him…and said, Understandest thou what thou readest? And he said, How can I, except some man should guide me? Then Philip opened his mouth, and began at the same Scripture, and preached unto him Jesus.. and the eunuch said, See, here is water, what doth hinder me to be baptized? And Philip said, If thou believest with all thine heart, thou mayest, And he answered and said, I believe that Jesus Christ is the Son of God.. and they went down both into the water, both Philip and the eunuch, and he baptized him

F = Faith (Confidence)

Anointing for acting on God's promises with confidence; believe and inspire others to believe, move forward when won't; inspiring, optimistic, trusting, and hopeful.

Hebrews 11:1-3 Now faith is the substance of things hoped for, the evidence of things not seen. For by it the elders obtained a good report. Through faith, we understand that the worlds were formed by the word of God so that things which are seen were not made of things which do appear.

G = Giving (Resource)

Anointing for giving money and resources for the work of the Lord cheerfully and liberally; may have the ability to make money, stewardship focus, disciplined, charitable, and resourceful.

> *Luke 21:1-4 And he looked up and saw the rich men casting their gifts into the treasury and he saw also a certain poor widow casting in thither two mites. And he said, Of a truth, I say unto you, that this poor widow hath cast in more than they all; for all these have of their abundance cast into the offerings of God but she of her penury hath cast in all the living that she had.*

H = Helps (Support)

Anointing for doing practical and necessary tasks which support and meet other's needs, serving behind the scenes, available, willing, loyal, and dependable.

> *Colossians 4:7-8 All my state shall Tychicus declare unto you who is a beloved brother, and a faithful minister and fellow servant in the Lord whom I have sent unto you for the same purpose, that he might know your estate, and comfort your hearts.*

HH = Hospitality (Acceptance)

Anointing for caring for people via a fellowship, food, shelter; creating a safe, comfortable environment where others feel welcome, friendly, gracious, inviting, and warm.

> *Acts 16:14-15 And a certain woman named Lydia, a seller of purple, of the city of Thyatira, which worshipped God, heard us whose heart the Lord opened, that she attended unto the things which were spoken of Paul. And when she was baptized, and her household, she besought us, saying, If ye have judged me to be faithful to the Lord, come into my house, and abide there And she constrained us.*

I = Intercession (Protection)

Anointing for praying consistently for others, and seeing frequent and specific results; feeling compelled to pray; awareness of spiritual leading and battles; and advocate, caring, sincere, and a peacemaker.

> *1 Timothy 2:1-2 I exhort therefore, that, first of all, supplications, prayers, intercessions, and quiet and peaceable life in all godliness and honestly*

K = Knowledge (Awareness)

Anointing for operating with a revelation of truth, unusual biblical insight, searching the scriptures, inquisitive, responsive, observant, insightful, reflective, studious, and truthful.

> *Mark 2:6-8 But there were certain of the scribes sitting there, and reasoning In their hearts, Why doth this man thus speak blasphemies? Who can forgive sins but God only? And immediately when Jesus perceived in his spirit that they so reasoned within themselves, he said unto them, Why reason ye these things in your hearts?*

L = Leadership (Direction)
Anointing for casting vision, motivating and directing people to fulfill God's purposes, presenting "big picture", establish goals, visionary, diligent, influential, and trustworthy.

> *Luke 22:25-26 And he said unto them, The kings of the Gentiles exercise lordship over them, and they that exercise authority upon them are called benefactors. But ye shall not be so but he that is greater among you, let him be as the younger and he that is chief, as he that doth serve.*

M = Mercy (Care)
Anointing for helping the suffering, needy or oppressed; expressing love, grace and dignity to those in hardship; empathetic, compassionate, sensitive, kind, and caring.

Matthew 5:7 Blessed are the merciful for they shall obtain mercy.

P = Prophecy (Conviction)

Anointing for revealing and proclaiming truth for understanding, correction, repentance or edification; exposing sin or deception; seeing and warning; discerning, outspoken, confronting, authoritative, convicting, and uncompromising.

2 Peter 1:19-21 We have also a more sure word of prophecy;...that no prophecy of the Scripture is of any private interpretation. For the prophecy came not in old time by the will of man but holy men of God spoke as they were moved by the Holy Ghost.

S = Shepherding (Nurture)

Anointing for nurturing, caring for and guiding people toward on-going spiritual maturity; discipling, protective, supportive, long-term relationships, and role modelling.

1 Peter 5:2,3 ...feed the flock of God which is among you, taking the oversight thereof, not by constraint, but willingly, not for filthy lucre, but of a ready mind, neither as being lords over God's heritage, but being examples to the flock

T = Teaching (Application)

Anointing for understanding clearly explaining applying God's Word and inspiring obedience; practical truths, disciplined, perceptive, teachable, authoritative analytical, and articulate.

> *Acts 18:24-28 And a certain Jew named Apollos, born at Alexandria, and eloquent man, and mighty in the Scriptures, came to Ephesus. This man instructed in the way of the Lord, and being fervent in the spirit, he spake and taught diligently the things of the Lord, knowing only the baptism of John. And he began to speak boldly in the synagogue whom when Aquila and Priscilla had heard, they took him unto them and expounded unto him the way of God more perfectly. And when he was disposed to pass into Achaia, the brethren wrote, exhorting the disciples to receive him who, when he was come, helped them much which had believed through grace. For he mightily convinced the Jews and that publicly, showing by the Scriptures that Jesus was Christ.*

W = Wisdom (Guidance)

Anointing for applying spiritual truth effectively to meet a need in a specific situation; seeing solution and consequences; sensible, insightful, wise, experienced, and practical.

> *James 3:17-18 But the wisdom that is from above is first pure, then peaceable, gentle, and easy to be entreated; full of mercy and good fruits, without partiality, and without hypocrisy. And the fruit of righteousness is sown in peace of them that make peace.*

REFERENCES

1. Hollinger, T. D. (n.d.). *Placing Christ at the Center of Christian Leadership Values* Thomas D. Hollinger. Retrieved from http://docplayer.net/11133399-Placing-christ-at-the-center-of-christian-leadership-values-thomas-d-hollinger.html

2. Maxwell, J. C. (2007). *The 21 irrefutable laws of leadership: follow them and people will follow you.* Nashville, TN: Thomas Nelson.

3. Ferch, S. R., & Spears, L. C. (2011). *The spirit of servant-leadership.* New York: Paulist Press, c2011

4. Hillman, J. (n.d.). *The Soul's Code.* Retrieved from https://www.personaltransformation.com/james_hillman.html

5. Robinson, H. W. (2014). *Biblical Preaching: The Development and Delivery of Expository Messages.* Grand Rapids: Baker Academic

6. Wilkinson, B. (2005). *The Seven Laws of the Learner How to Teach Almost Anything to Practically Anyone.* Multnomah.

ABOUT THE AUTHOR

Chris Scott is a Master Life Coach; to life coaches globally. For over 25 years, she has assisted Ministry Consultants and Pastors to help better coach their leadership team to serve more effectively. Chris has trained and certified over 450 life coaches globally. She is a Licensed and Ordained Minister at Tabernacle of Praise Church International, where she is Missions Director, training and leading missionaries to serve in the Nations. She is also a member of the leadership team of Living Sacrifice Prophetic Ministries in Trinidad and Tobago. She is a Missionary to Haiti, Belize, Jamaica, South Africa, Trinidad and Tobago and the Dominican Republic.

Chris is a three-time Author! Her first book, "*Discovering Your Spiritual Gifts Connecting the Dots to Your Purpose*" (first edition) that has blessed people globally. Her second book "*Treasures in My Heart*" is an anthology compiled of the stories by 12 amazing co-authors that made the Amazon Best Seller list and #1 New Release list. Her third book is titled "*Good Morning My Sister*" a daily devotional for women. Her first book is now available in stores and

Libraries in South Africa, Trinidad and Tobago, Bahamas, and throughout the United States.

In 2015 Chris received the honor of being presented with The President's Volunteer Service Award (PVSA), by President Barack Obama, which is a national recognition for her work in the community. She is a graduate of Jacksonville Theological Seminary, where she received a Bachelor of Arts degree in Theology and a Masters in Christian Psychology. She is also a graduate of Ohio Christian University and earned a bachelor's degree in interdisciplinary studies.

She has appeared on Fox 5 Atlanta, CBS 46 Atlanta Get Plugged In, Atlanta Live Channel 57 and several radio stations. In April 2020, Chris formed Coaching Forward International to help those coping with quarantine and COVID-19. The helpline was created to accept the call and coach the hurting to recovery through encouragement.

Chris Scott is married to her wonderful husband of 32 years and has 3 children, 4 grandchildren! She thanks God for her amazing family.

Thank you for reading my book! I pray that you found the keys to discovering your gifts! Please go to Amazon and leave a review to let others know how this book can also help them connect the dots to their purpose.

You can connect with me online at www.chrisscott.net

or via social media at authorchrisscott on facebook, twitter and instagram

Made in the USA
Monee, IL
19 December 2023

49813057R00094